We're Not Asking

'Beating Down the Great Obama Backlash'

Start the Revolution: www.werenotasking.com

By JM Bryson

Black Heart Publishing © 2015

Cover Photo: © Jose Inesta/Unsplash

Prologue

"Morality cannot be legislated, but behavior can be regulated. Judicial decrees may not change the heart, but they can restrain the heartless." – MLK

Eradicating the racism of a post-Obama era is a black thing. The only group of people that would call it a radical idea is comprised of white people who say the same thing, but brand it racist when it's said by black people. They are tone deaf to irony. They profess to hate Political Correctness, but offer no substitutes to it and whine about being called racist – which they don't consider 'politically correct.'

As with most black American media, this work offers a disclaimer, an ode to white people to suggest our hands are up and we aren't seeking to harm them. This is a different kind of revolution. We are simply going to work to fix a system that is broken for us. We don't intend to deport all of you; we don't hate you; you can keep your banks and credit scores, but we will be using different tools in the coming days. You still look pretty, OK?

But, Dear White People, understand that our respect and love for you as fellow citizens ends at the curb of our collective sacrifices. If you feel that you will be personally harmed by fair competition with a large and healthy black community, then, yes, you will be harmed. How that looks depends on you.

Still, make no mistake, there is a greater good served by a healthy black community. A fair America is a better America. If a better-qualified black girl beats out a white boy for a slot in medical school, the white boy and his family need to accept it – not 'white adjust' the system as has been done with the University of California admissions system and a million other social battlegrounds.

Ascendant black America invokes the most conservative of values: fairness. It's dispiriting that some, who are emotionally mired in the early 20th century, will consider a quest to remedy rampant unfairness as radical.

Best Way to Read This Book

The best way to read this book is to consider it open source code for black ascendance: Add your own brilliance and change any and all suggestions in these pages so they do the most good.

For those who don't know: "open source" computer code is written and then improved upon by groups of programmers. Code is simply the words, letters, numbers and other symbols that tell computers what to do. It is typed in using regular computer keyboards. One programmer comes up with an idea – for a videogame, an app, word processing software – and puts her skeletal code in front of a community of users. It's a collaborative effort.

The community adds, deletes and edits the words, letters, numbers and other symbols, making it more robust, responsive and able to do what Programmer #1 envisioned.

The other way to write code is also group-based. Technocrats like Bill Gates, Steve Jobs, Larry Ellison, Mark Zuckerberg – every software billionaire – hire teams to write the code that makes them rich. They supply the vision and the money and programmers are paid to make the idea work.

Success is also defined group-style. Lovers of Minecraft, digital cameras, YouTube, iPads, Facebook and other programming vote their approval with their dollars or time.

Group work is as old as humankind; it's at the heart of our earliest endeavors – farming, hunting, gathering; it was central to the Industrial Revolution – assembly lines, factory work; it made modern media possible – film studios, radio, television and print conglomerates – and now, it influences the Information Age.

The updated collaborative work model proved so productive that it spilled out of the computer science world and morphed into "crowd sourcing." Crowd sourcing is engaging a large number of people to contribute just a little, per person, to make a large project happen. It's not a new strategy, just reapplied – the Civil Rights Movement was crowdsourced.

Today, entire industries are based on crowd sourcing. The websites Kickstarter, IndieGoGo, GoFundMe and a hundred others make billions of dollars by helping people ask for help on thousands of products.

The core assumption is groups can quickly solve problems that would take much, much longer for even the most talented individuals. Microsoft Office, for example, has about 30 million lines of code, more than an individual could write in a decade. If the tech industry relied solely on talented individuals, we'd still be playing Pong. The Information Age is, by necessity, an age of collaboration.

So, the "source code" gets reworked by many minds and talents until it is an elegant batch of functional object code that can be sold on the open market or freely shared.

That is what this book provides and how you should read it: consider it a collection of source code-type ideas that require the brilliance of black Americans in order to thrive in the real world.

Still, there is a huge difference, between this type of "source code" and that of the tech industry. White collaboration is a greased wheel in America. Name virtually any industry group comprised mainly of white people and it's a certainty that both government and industry worked to ensure collaboration. White farmers were granted loans for seed, land and equipment from groups that could help them; white programmers sucked up virtually every dollar of tech venture capital to create new tech offerings, white bankers were given unprecedented leverage to expand their organizations.

Black Americans who attempt to organize are either starved out financially or attacked through media and other channels.

We are the Group that Must Forever Be Ungrouped. You don't have to believe these words, look up "New Black Panthers" on your internet search engine of choice and you will see thousands of comments that would lead you to believe that this poorly funded organization – a few dozen pro-black activists – are an American al-Qaeda. Then, search for "white lynch mobs" or "militias" as a comparison.

Certain white people experience palpable fear when black people look to collectively solve our own problems. They resort to fairy tales, saying with straight faces that every white success story was a solo triumph, with no help from the white community at all.

That is the best reason EVER to do something. When the hand that holds you down is connected to the mouth that outright lies to you, offering to solve your problems – use your feet and get far away.

This book is an instruction manual for the doers and deep thinkers that have come to a near-Kennedyesque conclusion: 'Ask not what I can do for my country … after what my country's done to me.'

There are big solutions in here for big problems and the details have been glossed over. That is intentional. You don't have to know the name of every black person wrongfully executed by racist cops to know there is a problem.

Activism, like programming, has to be intentional and with a destination in mind. One considers the obstructions, potential solutions, desired outcome and gets there with actual effort.

We have been blinded to these simple facts for generations by forced poverty, terrorism and propaganda to keep us from a constructive unity.

The quest for black ascendance, which simply means having society work as well for us as it does now for white people, is simple.
Do it together. Do it now.

There will be resistance, but if we can't accept that, then slavery isn't dead. Anything worthwhile has an element of conflict in it.

The resistance we will face isn't even complicated. Certain white people don't want to lose their privilege. That is it. It is no more or less complicated than that.

But, that is where our open source code paradigm can save us. In the coding community, people do great work and then run out of steam. Other people step in where those people faltered and achieve the next step. One person steps up, then another and another until the goal is achieved. Failure begets success; success begets failure, until an ultimate success is realized.

Dr. Martin Luther King, Jr.'s assassination was the most blatant example of how white America deals with black collectivism. They attack the head. Fortunately, the Civil Rights Movement was more than one man. Still, old habits die hard. Many white people see President Obama as the head of a movement to unite black people through pride.

So, they indulge in character assassination.

We cannot allow that to happen. This book wants to ensure we keep our eyes wide open.

Most of us read books passively, we let the authors' ideas wash over us and set them aside for the rest of our lives. This book doesn't exist without action and this prologue suggests how to convert words into action.

One of the most successful human endeavors in recent history is digitizing information. It has taught us how to think logically, forced us to eliminate the extraneous, showed us how to establish effective workflows and made us plan for multiple contingencies. Using the lessons of software programming, we can attack our societal problems.

How Computer Programmers Develop Source Code
John Saunders, writing on stackoverflow.com wrote about what constitutes an effective development plan for programmers:

"You can provide an overview, which will summarize some of what you need to do. But, as you explore the requirements, the users will discover things, learn, and change their mind. Revising the plan. As you explore the technology, the developers will discover things, learn, and revise the plan.

It can't be that hard – people do this all the time.

"The plan's audience is management. Managers want a 'reasonably' detailed description of all the activities. As the users and developers learn about the requirements and the technology, the details change. This makes the 'reasonable' test very, very hard to satisfy. When the details change constantly, what level of detail is 'reasonable'?

"Changes to the plan can (and do) arrive on a daily basis. Most managers won't want to make daily changes to the plan. So, too much detail becomes 'unreasonable.' In order to create a plan that doesn't change very often, the plan actually needs to be a summary of activities. The only workable version of a software development plan is a series of goals defined – not in terms of activities – in terms of functionality to be released to users.

"In short, people do it **badly** all the time. In 30+ years of software development (much of it as a military subcontractor) there is a fantasy about planning that is simply not born out by the facts. Projects are cancelled with "reasonably detailed" plans, overly detailed plans and no plan at all.

"Indeed, a plan is often the leading cause of cancellation. Why? With a 'reasonably detailed' list of activities, any learning means the plan is wrong. Since the plan diverges from actual execution something must be wrong.

"Toss a coin. If you deem that execution is wrong, cancel the project for not following the plan. If you deem the plan is wrong, fix the plan to match the real world. The more detailed the plan, the more it seems 'right' and the more likely to deem execution as faulty.

"Bottom line, a software development plan can be a fantasy document written as part of a … development methodology in which all kinds of things are over-specified up front and changes (from learning as the team progresses) [are] punished.

"Or, a software development plan is an agile [document] that simply shows the sprints to be completed. The 'reasonable' level of detail is actually quite low – it's just a summary. And, it changes during each [review]."

We Can't Afford White Guilt

Now, you know how to read the book and have taken as much "source code" comparison as you can stand. The next big issue to be aware of is dealing with the toxicity of white guilt.

There are millions of dead white ancestors and millions of more living white people who should feel guilty for their contributions to 'Jim Slavery' (the government-backed economic subjugation of black people from the dawn of slavery to the sunset of Jim Crow) but the problem with any type of guilt is the one feeling guilty has some responsibility to the other party.

In Obama's and post-Obama America, there is precious little responsibility to be seen from most white people. And, while we wait for these phantoms to speak up and acknowledge the true intents of their actions, black America positions itself as powerless, in need of being made whole. Worse, we expect white guilt to be an engine of rectification. The facts are on our side, but psychology is not.

A guilty party's first statement when caught is, 'I can't undo it.' Be it murder, embezzling, rape or genocide. The mea culpa lowers the bar and defies anyone to ask for more than they are willing to give.

White guilt won't give us full citizenship. That must be snatched from their hands. Until and unless they roll back the U.S. Constitution to directly enslave us, we must take what is ours. And, even if they codify slavery again, we possess the power to veto it.

They are responsible, but we have the means to repair ourselves. Their guilt won't stop them from trying to sabotage such efforts, so what kind of guilt is it, really? It's the guilt of a serial philanderer who says, 'No more' as he heads to another illicit affair. The syllables of their regret are soap bubbles.

Table of Contents

Chapter 1
Civil War IV

"We are a nation with no geographic boundaries" -
*– 'Pledge,' **Janet Jackson***

If you are black and struggling to pay your bills, despite working hard and pursuing your education there is good news and bad news. The bad news is the main reason you are not where you need to be financially is that you are trapped on a battlefield in the middle of a war. This war was declared years before you, your parents or grandparents were even born, and it still continues.

The war is Civil War IV and it is being fought by a disgruntled group of racists who refuse to accept black people as their equals. This war has raged for 150 years; once as a hot war, then as a terror-based police action to destroy the equalizing effects of Reconstruction, and a third time as a cold war in the mid-20th century with the Civil Rights Movement of Dr. Martin Luther King.

The signature victory for racists was when they turned back equality during Civil War II – Reconstruction. That was a brief time when black people, by law, were granted access to society in the same measure as whites. White and Black Americans would very likely be economic equals today if Reconstruction had been allowed to run its course. But, the Sons of the South, traitors to the US, wouldn't let institutionalized racism die. And, their victory in Civil War II transformed into Jim Crow laws, housing, job, educational, financial and law enforcement discrimination that continues to this day.

Describing these battles as war is frightening because of the implications of mass death. But, it's not hyperbole. Black towns were burned to the ground, thousands of black men, women and children were lynched by terrorists, black women were raped, black economies were squashed or stolen, black education was compromised and black men were jailed and driven out of their homes. And, today, unarmed black men are being gunned down by police, our voting rights are being stripped and our homes and livelihoods are being stolen.

All of this has happened with the informed consent of the American legal system. That's how war works. Murder, rape, theft, detainment, torture and terrorism are legalized and used against an enemy. Bombs are just exclamation points.

It is war. Don't make the fatal mistake of believing otherwise. It is the continuation of a generations-long struggle for a good people to be free and unharmed by evil elements of government and society. American government is quick to war – even the NASA space program was war-based. American generals wanted to have the ultimate vantage point and planned on detonating nukes on the moon as a show of force. The CIA is always at war; the drugs the CIA flooded into black American neighborhoods funded just one of thousands of its deadly battles. America wages war on many levels: physical, financial, environmental and psychological.

Psychological operations play a central role in the Sons of the South's all-out assault on black people. By forcing black Americans to see everything through the eyes of white Americans, they win by pretending there is no war against black Americans.

Howard Bryant of ESPN wrote, "…in a fractured country desperate for racial victories, integration appears to be a universal triumph, but its implementation crippled the black infrastructure. Affluent black families, freed from segregation, bank and government redlining, dispersed. Integration arrived in the major leagues but Negro Leagues owners and executives were not invited, and a black-owned industry collapsed."

So, we accept curiosities large and small, such as the well-known experiment that "shows" job applicants with black-sounding names are far less likely to be hired for jobs, sight unseen.

It is curious because we assume that only white people are in charge of hiring. It is also curious that, each year, members of some black organization will rend their garments because there are so few black faces on our favorite TV programs or in feature films. Or, we will hear an unfiltered comment from a white person, like New York Times writer Alessandra Stanley who called black television producer Shonda Rhimes an "angry black woman" because of the strong black female characters she creates.

The reason for the history lesson is because it's about to repeat itself. Call it the Great Obama Backlash. Over the course of President Obama's tenure, racists managed to shape the conversation about race in as slick a fashion as oil companies shaped environmental policy under George W. Bush. Their efforts were expensive and remarkable. They absolved racists, vilified those subjected to racism, framed black people as America's "only" racists, turned a nation against its leader and won federal elections with little more than a Tea Party oath to 'sabotage the black guy.' They supplanted black people, in white America's minds, with gay people and Latinos/Hispanics and, as ever, planted seeds of doubt about black Americans' intellectual capacities.

They have weaponized race.

Weapons have been anything the Sons of the South could lay their hands on. Guns and knives, of course, but also ropes, chemicals, trucks, legislation, psychology, schoolbooks, welfare, television, movies, radio, magazines and the internet. But, their nuclear weapon has always been blocking access to jobs, both indirectly, by being champions of inferior education, and directly, by not hiring black people.

They enhance their small numbers by enticing the useful idiots who espouse racism on their behalf.

Today, racists are using President Obama to turn white public opinion against black people. They are so emboldened that actor Ben Stein can blithely proclaim President Obama as "the most racist president in US history," ignoring Calvin Coolidge's well-documented hatred of black people and actual slave-owning presidents. By "racist," what Stein and other like-minded white people mean is President Obama doesn't accept white supremacy.

Americans of all colors should take note of the depth to which racists will sink.

CNN columnist Paul Waldman wrote:

Bashing President Obama for doing his job "was extremely astute and executed to near perfection. [Senate Minority Leader Mitch] McConnell understood well that the President gets credit when Washington works and blame when it doesn't – whether he deserves it in either case. So Republicans could pour sand in the gears of government and watch Obama suffer for it.

"And, it worked."

"What was the result of six years of unprecedented filibusters, debt ceiling crises, a government shutdown, 50 futile Affordable Care Act repeal votes, endless conspiracy theory theorizing and a dramatic increase in general buffoonery? Republicans took the House in 2010 and [in 2014] have taken the Senate."

The very things the Sons of the South warned about during slavery – the dishonesty and laziness of black people – is inbred into their own descendants. They have lied, cheated and stopped doing their jobs in order to make a black man look bad. They are the new Stepin Fetchits.

What is amazing is the cognitive dissonance it requires to be so racist. Skin color is a physical trait, not a behavior. There are white people who share identical views with some black people and vice versa. Still, black people have been systemically denied full rights because of skin color. On every societal indicator, we are lagging and some white people hate us for those failures and, using the President as an example, hate us for our successes in overcoming them.

It is the exact same mindset slavers had. No black achievement was due to black people's efforts, but every failing was in their nature. Our ancestors made them rich, individually and collectively, and they despised them for that.

Racists and apologists will tell you, slavery was a long time ago. They'll say, "I never owned a slave." But, U.S. laws of inheritance make a lie of that argument. Old money powers the American elite at this very minute. Slave labor, immigrant labor and child labor all contributed to the old money and upper middle class economic base; money that is still being spent today. Such exploitation is part of the reason most one-percenters are so wealthy. That money bought land, housing, businesses, respectability and inclusion while black people were forced into a post-slavery subsistence.

We couldn't buy housing during those times. Even if we did scrimp and save money against all odds, we couldn't buy the best housing. Our great-grandparents sharecropped to feed and clothe hungry families, with nothing left over to bequeath to their children. There was no financial legacy forthcoming. They were robbed of more than a trillion dollars worth of generational wealth.

Why so much hatred? Who is this reviled enemy these particular white people spent 15 generations of American history trying to destroy?: Your father. Your brother. Your uncle. Your cousin. Your son.

The black male.

The battles were both large and small, but the goal was the same. Anything that could disrupt the black male's family, diminish his earning power and denigrate his contribution to society was fair game.

It was death by a thousand cuts and it was insidious. It targeted black men, their women and families. It was a strategy of emasculation and erasure:

- **Courageous black soldiers who fought and died for America were not given credit for their military involvement**. They were paid less. When allowed to fight, they were more often assigned to high-fatality battles. In one example, out of thousands, the all-black 369th Infantry Regiment, nicknamed the Harlem Hellblazers, served a six-month tour of duty, the longest deployment of any unit in World War I. Ferocious and feared by the Germans because they fought until death instead of capture, the regiment served alongside the French army and won medals for combat valor from France. In May of 1918, privates Lincoln Johnson and Needham Roberts fought off a 24-man German patrol, though both were severely wounded. Johnson was the first American to receive the *Croix de Guerre* awarded by the French government, an award signifying extraordinary valor. By the end of the war, 171 members of the 369th were awarded the Legion of Honor or the Croix De Guerre. Despite the fact that they were decorated heroes returning to New York, men of the 369th Regiment were not allowed to participate in the Victory Parade of 1919. White military police back in the U.S. were ***ordered*** not to salute them.

- **Black people could not be depicted positively in popular culture** – white singer Van Morrison was told to change the name of his song from "Brown-Skinned Girl" to "Brown Eyed Girl." Comic book writer Jim Shooter was ordered by comic book editor Julius Schwartz to change the race of Ferro Lad, his new superhero, after Shooter made the character black. Movies with performers such as Lena Horne or the Nicholas Brothers had to film them so they could be easily cut out of the movies for Southern white audiences.

- **Black people couldn't buy homes.** Banks refused to loan money to black people and real estate codicils, such as in Edina, Minnesota, prohibited Realtors ™ from selling to black families.

- **Even today, shows like 'Mad Men' incite racism** by romanticizing an advertising culture that presently excludes black people to almost the same degree it did back in the 1960s.

- **The tech industry, a nursery for the next generation of billionaires, has done everything short of passing its own Jim Crow laws to exclude black men**. From venture capital, to hiring, to its advertising campaigns, it is a celebration of whiteness. With the rise of the new tech titans, the Bay Area home to Silicon Valley has grown much whiter in its demographics, a reverse of America's current demographic trend.

Today, with a black president in office and a black attorney general as the No. 1 law enforcement official, racists have reached the final frontier. Taking a cue from anti-black Fox News programming, Sons of South and their adherents now proclaim that only black people are racist:

- Cliven Bundy, who insists black people were better off as slaves in the U.S., says he's not racist.

- Donald Sterling, disgraced NBA owner who refused to rent his residential properties to black people and didn't want black people attending his team's games, says he's not racist.

- Mississippi teen-ager Deryl Dedmon who intentionally ran over and killed an innocent, middle-aged black stranger with his truck, calling him a "nigger" all the while, says he's not racist.

In their Southern-addled minds, the only existing racists are black people who call them on their racist behaviors. If you drop this book this very second and never learn another thing from it, take this lesson to heart: that is a final solution that cannot be allowed.

It is a slap in the faces of your ancestors, to blame their children for the evils of the children of slavers. If your only contribution to race relations is shutting down anyone who spouts that nonsense, you are honoring your family and the concept of truth.

There may come a time when black people can accurately be described as racists. It will arrive when brave black people accept the challenge of these pages and actually empower themselves. Power determines racism. There are no anti-white laws in America – not one. No white-owned farms were snatched, as in Zimbabwe, and given to black farmers. When black power is institutionalized, only then will black racism be possible. The war will be won. It will be up to those living in our future to decide whether to return centuries-old hatred with hate. Our task, here in the present, is to fight and win so they may make their decision.

Here are the stakes. Civil War IV is a war of large against small, hate against survival. It is the story of white men declaring war on black men, using the ancient Roman imperial military strategy of "divide and conquer" to separate black males from their strongest supporters – loving black families. Even after slavery's end, black men were forced away from their families by the rules of welfare; they received jail time for using illicit means to support their loved ones; while the white criminals who sold drugs to them in bulk did so with impunity.

All of these separation strategies were economically-focused. Welfare pushed black women into a new, lonely position of raising children with no fathers and little money. Like sharecroppers, they fought just to survive. Men in jail couldn't support wives and children; drug addiction switched off their paternal instincts and broke the circuits of being caring fathers.

These absent fathers taught their sons and daughters that black men don't stay in the home. An entire generation of black men and women, born in the 1950s and through the 2000s, bore the scars of broken families. After 150 years of war, the intact black family is a rarity – fewer than one in three black children have both a father and mother in the home.

Instead, black America has The Breeder. The man who fashions nests by making babies with multiple women in an effort to have places to land and then leave. It is a broken method to create family for those who never knew an intact home. And, it engenders another generation of children without fathers.

It is only on the shoulders of the amazing black women of our country that we have survived. Without them, we would have lost the war long ago. Our superwomen fed, clothed, housed and taught generations of us while the men were gone and never came back. They pulled from within themselves the power to be mothers, fathers, friends and trouble detectors. They kept most young black men alive when society desperately wanted to turn them into corpses.

And, they forgave like Jesus. Black men tore their hearts apart and they turned their collective cheeks and moved forward.

So, it is no surprise that black women are outpacing black men in earnings. They have been battle-tested. They deserve that money; they earned that money. They should continue to gain economic equality and black men will have to deal with that reality.

Still, both black men and women should understand that an agenda lies behind the deserved and hard-fought economic rise of the black woman.

In the economic battles of Civil War IV, black males are the true target. Hiring and promotion of black women are blurred and melded into gender issues. Generally, white and Asian males earn the most, white females earn the next most, black females earn less than that – and black males bring up the rear.

A saturation point is nearing. Soon, white women will narrow the gap between their salaries and those of white men. When white women earn close to what white men earn, the pay gap will stop being discussed. The media will trumpet, "Men and women finally earn equal pay for equal work!"

That illusory equity will put race – and black men – on the back burner of wage fairness efforts. In the eyes of white men, this is an act of economic castration: the current narrative will continue and be even more powerful: 'Black men can't support their families and should be considered less than men.'

That can't change in the current economic system. And, in the future? Even after racial and ethnic demographics tip in 2045 and white Americans become minorities, the Sons of the South have a plan. They have been busy setting up a new version of Old South Africa – a white, minority-run nation for the future. They want to ensure that their children, and only their children, are in power. It's why they are busy slandering black people as the "only American racists." It's why they keep black men away from positions of power and money. Eradicating racism erases their vision for the future. They never, ever want a meritocracy.

Again, black women deserve every penny they earn and more. But, with pay equity focused on gender alone, the bludgeon will have fallen on black men and the prospect of two healthy incomes and an intact family is pushed further away – and, not always by external forces.

Some black men resent women earning more than they earn; some women resent black men who earn less. So, 'divide and conquer' claims more victims while the true oppressor is untouched.

The reality is that even with the incrementally increasing wealth of black women, our collective financial net worth in the midst of Civil War IV is still miniscule relative to what it would be without racist intervention. Most of us try to survive with individual net worths on the order of a nickel of black wealth compared to a dollar of white wealth; that's $20,000 compared to $400,000.

By any economic measure, our quest for social equality has been a failure; our success is throw-away, based on how easily it's been depleted. Hundreds of thousands of our men and superwomen were washed away from middle class by the Great Recession and without the strategies of this book, many will never recover.

In America, wealth takes seed money (inheritance or family gifts) patience and connections. Black America has had only pockets of wealth – the Madame CJ Walkers, the Oprahs, the Robert and Sheila Johnsons. Even with a couple of billionaires, that is far too little wealth to raise 45 million boats, so we are seriously disadvantaged by a lack of connections. Numerically, we require a small town of Oprah Winfreys – about 1500 of her – to approximate white wealth at the highest-of-the-high end of the financial spectrum for our 45 million strong nation. And, that's only the billionaire class; that doesn't touch on the upper middle class millionaires and a solid middle class. We have no seed money.

And, the problem with patience is it requires a comfortable base. Looking for *another* job means having a job in the first place. Many black people are on the edge of hunger, eviction, desperation. Many of us react not because we don't have patience, but because we don't have the luxury of a solid base. College savings are extremely rare, inheriting a home is rare, being brought into a family business with employees and generations of sales is rare. As the song goes, our papas were rolling stones. All they left us was alone.

That is not the case for many white people. American industry has been transformed by Civil War IV into white industry. Our attempts to fully engage in the U.S. economy have moved slowly because we have been unable to overcome the layers of wives, brothers, sons, daughters, sisters, uncles, cousins and well-connected friends who are allowed to cut in line for jobs, promotions, loans, housing. They have connections. We can only maneuver on the fringe – until we control industries.

That won't happen until we conquer one collective psychological shortcoming: we must stop fearing the naked power grab. The power grab is a mainstay of white society from the plunder of native civilizations to the creation of corporate banana republics to the scorched earth competitiveness of Microsoft – "Buy 'em all off and let God sort 'em out."

We have far too few success stories because too few of us are accustomed to wrenching power out of the hands of others. That needs to change.

No.

It *has* to change.

The Good News

And, here – finally – is the good news. We can. We absolutely can. We 45 million black Americans can control industries. Taking a page from candidate Obama, the ability to do great things has always been in front of us. What has been missing is the will to collectively act instead of individually react.

Wars are not won accidentally. The reason this war rages on is that our only viable, unified opposition to the Sons of the South was the Civil Rights Movement, which formed some 90 years after the first Civil War. It's noteworthy that there were only 15 million black people alive in the U.S. at the start of that movement and 135 million white people, so we were much fewer in number and a smaller percentage of the overall population. We were even more outnumbered and outgunned than today. Still, our forefathers and mothers forged an amazing victory and then declared a ceasefire. But, the dismantling of Reconstruction during Civil War II should have taught us better about declaring victory too soon.

War is still being waged on us, yet many of us don't believe it despite all the signs: murders, economic destruction, innocent prisoners, targeted strikes, spies, military justice. Those are not accidents. One Trayvon Martin might be a tragic accident – but state legislatures clamoring to write laws allowing it to happen is casus belli for a very particular target.

Still, the war can be won, once and for all, by doing something that has been forbidden for us – uniting. There are 45 million of us. That's more than our largest, most prosperous state – California. Our economy is worth more than $1.1 TRILLION dollars. That's the 16th largest economy in the world, just a tick behind South Korea and Mexico. Nations like China, South Africa, Russia and Canada would bend over backwards to trade with us if we were a sovereign state.

With collective will, we can engage in a morally correct war against a centuries-old system of oppression and win outright. World history is peppered with much smaller and/or poorer countries prevailing against rich and powerful nations, including our own: Afghanistan versus Russia, Vietnam versus America, Russia versus Nazi Germany and, of course, the American Colonies versus England.

The precedent is there. Victory can be had. The missing ingredient is a collective will to fight for the right thing. To make it happen, a critical mass of our 45 million – not most, maybe not even many – has to counter two powerful psychological principles. One, of course, is the very effective psycho-political technique of divide-and-conquer. The other is the concept of "learned helplessness."

In **learned helplessness** studies, an animal is repeatedly exposed to an aversive stimulus which it cannot escape. Eventually, the animal stops trying to avoid the stimulus and behaves as if it is **helpless** to change the situation.

Learned helplessness in the psychology lab is demonstrated by putting rats into a container of water with the burners slowly raising the temperature to dangerous levels. Rats will fight against drowning at first, but as their situation gets dire, they "normalize" their plight, not recognizing the true danger – boiling to death. They will die without fighting back, even if escape routes are introduced.

Many Americans, not just us, have learned to be helpless. Women give up on their dreams of business success, poor people give up trying to move beyond their circumstances and old people sigh and say, "That's just the way it is."

Learned helplessness explains many self-defeating behaviors of the black community. For instance, the 'Crabs in a Barrel' mindset works in conjunction with systemic racism to make it doubly effective.

The absolute best cop in the world is the one that's been planted in your mind. It will tell you to make fun of your classmates for 'acting white.' It will say, 'Find a sucker, bump his head.' It will forge better "nigger killers" than the KKK could ever dream, as if the Klan of old crafted an army of young black drones that are brutally killing their targets and building more drones.

Is this behavior predicated on centuries of racism and oppression? Yes. Does that excuse its consequences? No.

Society is a social agreement, not a cement wall. Behaviors can be changed and are changed. It's done all the time. In the words of Wyclef Jean of the Fugees: 'If you let a muthafucka kick you three times, he'll kick you three times. If you let him kick you two times, he'll kick you two times. If you let him kick you one time, he'll kick you one time. But, if you break off his leg, won't be no kickin' going on.'

Behaviors of oppressors can be modified. Japan was once considered one of history's most aggressive, war-prone states. Today, they don't have a functional army. Closer to home, the Civil Rights Movement changed hearts and minds in a huge way. Racists are no longer widely and openly tolerated.

The only downside with how black America won against its oppressors during the Civil Rights Movement is we essentially borrowed the tools used to effect change.

Borrowed tools have to be returned.

The Civil Rights Movement was a heady, harrowing time for black people. Thousands upon thousands of us were killed in its name – most without lifting a fist in defense. But, change happened. Our grandparents and parents stood toe-to-toe with the Sons of the South, unarmed, and won amazing victories.

It was incredible, one of the most transformative moments in human history. Pure bravery. Major changes were made to America's civil rights laws at the height of its global power and paranoia – and only one side was truly armed. That is virtually unprecedented.

Our Civil Rights Movement used U.S. media to tell its stories; it pleaded its case to the U.S. Courts; it counted on U.S. law enforcement for protection, it expected the U.S. President and Congress to pass Civil Rights laws.

The victories remain historic for black people, brown people, women, immigrants, gay people, disabled people and more. But, the victories for black people weren't sustainable without a black-owned infrastructure. By comparison, white women have benefited tremendously because they collectively possessed the infrastructure, by virtue of their relationships with white men, to sustain growth.

Would any reasonable person say the U.S. Courts and law enforcement, up to and including the Obama administration, have been pro-black? Those borrowed mechanisms, especially the courts, snapped back. It's not a coincidence that both the courts and law enforcement went on a jailing spree a decade after the end of the Civil Rights Era. Ronald Reagan, a man notorious for hating black people, was the face of the racially-based war on drugs and white people adored him for it. The world had never seen such peacetime mass jailings. Again, the black male was the target.

Borrowed tools were back in their owners' hands. And, boy! Were they pissed!

It's not the fault of our foremothers and forefathers who fought for Civil Rights. They couldn't envision a realistic aftermath of their efforts, because it was something they had never experienced. Many of them expected to die before seeing any appreciable change. All they could imagine was that, somehow, equality would fix everything.

They couldn't anticipate the permanent resentment of certain white people, white people who saw their racial hatred being outed by other white people as character flaws. Our forefathers and foremothers could never have comprehended that hatred's depth. These Sons and Daughters of the South did not want black people to have *anything* – no money, no jobs, no homes, no votes, no say. Every bit of social infrastructure controlled by black people was a slap in their faces. Sound familiar?

These racists had a plan up their sleeves. They knew wars don't end with the last bullet. Countless conflicts, including World War II, taught them that nation-building was the next step after the guns were silenced. They knew equality couldn't work if one side went home to clean, comfortable, safe homes and well-paid jobs and one side was forced to rent in neighborhoods where drugs had been introduced and the pursuit of subsistence was always top-of-mind. That was the dystopia they labored to create for black people.

Wars like Civil War IV have been fought before. There are blueprints for victory and beyond that a select few groups have created. One other group, historically, has dealt with this kind of manic hatred – Jewish people.

Many of the same lies and prejudices attributed to black people have been applied to Jews throughout much of history – they were called dirty, stupid, smelly, lazy, dishonest, ugly, suited to slavery. To show the analogy isn't that much of a stretch, Jewish people were even considered by some to be genetically better at playing basketball back in the 1930s and 1940s, the same way young black people are viewed today.

Wall Street Journal reporter Jonathan Sacks wrote about anti-Semitism in January 2015 in a way that illuminates parallels between the hatreds experienced by the black and Jewish communities:

"Anti-Semitism becomes deadly only when a culture, nation or faith suffers from a cognitive dissonance so profound that it becomes unbearable. It happens when the way the group sees itself is contradicted by the way it is seen by the world. It is a symptom of an unendurable sense of humiliation.

"Christianity, which had been transformed by the conversion of the Roman Emperor Constantine in the fourth century, found itself overtaken by Islam in the 11th century. Germany, which had seen itself as the supreme nation in Europe, was defeated in World War I and then punished under the Treaty of Versailles.

"These humiliations resulted not in introspection but in a search for foreign culprits – for external enemies who could be blamed and destroyed. The parallel in Islam over the past century was the defeat and dissolution of its one remaining bastion of imperial power, the Ottoman Empire, in 1922. Six years later, radical political Islam was born in Egypt in the form of the Muslim Brotherhood.

"Hate cultivated for such cultural and political ends resolves the dissonance between past glory and current ignominy. By turning the question 'What did we do wrong?' into 'Who did this to us?' it restores some measure of self-respect and provides a course of action. In psychiatry, the clinical terms for this process are splitting and projection; it allows people to define themselves as victims."

Over the years, the Jewish community learned from the behaviors Sacks describes to win its own conflict against its haters. Sadly, it took a hot war and the murder of six million Jews to galvanize that community.

But, the template is there. The work has been done and the results are in. A successful social blueprint for a thriving black society can be had by borrowing strategy from the winning battles of Jewish society. Just as Egypt stole knowledge from Kemet and Rome stole from Egypt and Greece stole from Rome and on and on to America stealing from England, our concepts of societies are cobbled-together inventions that either work and remain or don't work and are discarded.

Today, American Jews are among the wealthiest and best educated people in the U.S. The same applies to gay white men and Asian Americans. Their common link is they are considered minorities. They even have ghettos – Skokie, IL, Fire Island, NY. All of these ghettos are upscale with million-dollar homes with swimming pools and private security forces.

But, if you say the word "minority" to the average white person, images of black people and worn-out neighborhoods in Detroit spring to mind. Instead of educated, affluent and powerful, the phrase "minority," as applied to black people, evokes ignorance, poverty and weakness.

Bullshit.

Black America is too complex to be pigeonholed into those negative stereotypes. The only failing of modern Black America is that it doesn't it totally control its image. The reality is it is a juggernaut. It is comprised of some of the most powerful and smartest people in the world – President Obama and his wife Michelle, Neil DeGrasse Tyson, Oprah Winfrey, Tiger Woods, Philip Emeagwali, Michael Jordan, Robert Johnson, Jay-Z and Beyonce, Ken Chenault, Lonnie Johnson, Eric Holder and millions upon millions more.

Where we often stumble is in our underestimation of America as a screen-based nation. America gets its news, information, love, sustenance and attitude from screens – computer, movie, smartphone, and television. It is there that the juggernaut falters.

You think BET is black-owned? Think again. Black women own the majority of Essence.com? That was never the case. For every Tyler Perry Studios and OWN, there are 1,000 white-owned media production companies.

Positive media coverage was one of the battles that 20th century black America thought it won, but eventually lost. It certainly got good press from the white media around the middle of the 20th century. But, because it didn't create its own media army, those stories turned bad and the 21st century image war was lost.

Still, media is simply a crucial piece of a larger need.

Now – in the early 21st century – is the time to fix long-standing problems of being treated as "others." Our Jewish twin community also has a history of being denied human rights and being shut out of economic systems. But, despite that – and the fact that there are more than 10 times as many black people as Jewish people – they are thriving financially and educationally. One of the most brilliant collective strategies of the Jewish people was embedding themselves in American media.

They owned the industry and told their stories. Jewishness was normalized. Shmutz, shlep, plotz and meshugener were implanted into non-Jewish minds.

Still, it's not a perfect fit. We don't have the same level of access to media. Also, Jews were quick to accept the post-slavery concept of whiteness and some of them joined in to oppress black people. Further, as much as anti-Semites like to call Jews a race, they are not. Should they choose, the majority of them could easily pass for gentile white people – as many do.

And, Jews are bound to their religion, which is an obvious organizer for any social movement. But, black people have no single religion and our church filters are no longer in sync: What Rev. TD Jakes supports might not pass muster with Minister Farrakhan.

While religion can and should be part of the organizing process, its time at the head of the table, its Civil Rights Movement role, has long passed. That alone sets the new black resurgence apart from the Jewish struggles.

The Jewish blueprint is a good starting point, but not perfect for black people. It needs an update. One obvious source of inspiration is a population that shares a number of social issues with black America – the Mexican American community. Not the entire Hispanic community, just the Mexican American community.

We deal with many of the same issues. Often, Mexican Americans are pushed into lower wage jobs, buffeted by the violence of drug traffickers, blocked from viable higher education and are generally cornered into hard, paycheck-to-paycheck lives that shorten the horizons for their children and force them to scale back their dreams.

But, pockets of Mexican Americans have been able to succeed in a land where a small, vocal segment hates them and wants them to return to their country of origin. Go back to Africa? Go back to Mexico? Two sides of the same racism.

Like black people, they are not homogenous – Mexico City residents do not see the world precisely as those from Michoacan do – but strangers in a strange land cope with the realities of their situations. Mexican Americans – a notable example being Cesar Chavez – have learned to cooperate in order to collectively rise.

One of the most important common bonds the two groups share is that progressive white people understand that bigotry stunted the natural growth of both communities.

Affirmative Action and the Civil Rights Movement targeted the inequities black people faced in the U.S., but before any other groups, white women, gays, the disabled and veterans, members of the Mexican American community were also placed under those protections.

If black people are the first adopters of modern U.S. Civil Rights, the second wave was the Mexican American community.

With Jewish and Mexican American strategy combined with our own unique successes, we have more than a fighting chance to take our rightful place as leaders of 21st century America.

What is necessary is a collective will, a plan and cooperation. This book will offer up a blueprint, but it is simply a receptacle for the genius of black people.

When you consider how hard they tried to kill us off, to take away our hope and to make us doubt ourselves, it's a miracle we don't all have PTSD. Our existence, as flawed as it is, is a testament to black genius, to the wisdom of survivors. That genius is the engine of our ascendance.

We have survived and now we should plan to thrive. It's wonderful to have thousands of black millionaires and three or four black billionaires, but as the economic crisis of 2008 proved, millions of hard-working black people aren't on stable financial footing. Homes and jobs were lost and "middle class" turned out to be an illusion for us. If we take care of the business at hand, not only is there potential for substantially more millionaires and billionaires, but working class people can actually make a living, raise healthy families and pursue their happiness – just like most white people. That is a definition for thriving.

Wars aren't won by accident; success can't be sustained by accident.

As the late, great poet and proto-rapper Gil Scott Heron said on his "Message to the Messengers," "… if they really knew the truth, why would they tell you?"

We are in this on our own. We must create a new strategy and the model for success is nothing like it was back in 1955. Back then, you knew most white people hated you and didn't believe in your equality. Then, you needed a Dr. King, a Malcolm X, a Rosa Parks, a Stokely Carmichael as the charismatic leader of your organization.

Today, we know that many such charismatic leaders are assassinated or co-opted, something that cannot be put past any post-Obama administration.

Today's leaders should group together, with clear common goals and an understanding that simply not being lynched isn't the Promised Land. Having common goals and clear remedies makes it easier to navigate in an era when more white people believe in ghosts than racism.

In the eyes of millions of white people, there are no white racists; that's because racism isn't as pronounced as in 1955. Instead of being legally protected, it lives in the gray area of doubt. Are there more black men in prison because of the moral failings of the black race? Are there fewer black scientists because black people aren't as intelligent? Are black people genetically predisposed to violence? All of these questions have answers that can be linked to generations of racism. For racists, they are important questions, because they obscure any resolution. For instance, if black people are genetically predisposed to violence, the only solution available to white society is to lock black people up as quickly as possible.

Racism isn't racism. Not anymore. Now, it's *racisms*. It's situational and partially hidden by other agendas. For example, it's easy to call Republicans racist for trying to block voting by black voters, but there are some white Republicans who see it purely as a numbers game. Instead of black people, they see Democratic voters they want to prevent from helping their opponents.

Politicians do that each and every day. When he was running for the House of Representatives, Barack Obama, like an OG, worked hard to block the votes of those who might support his opponent.

Just win, baby.

Modern racism provides cover for more virulent racists by larding them in with white people with other, non-racial agendas: the number-focused Republican in the example above stands side by side with the Republican who hates black people with every fiber of his being.

Since modern racism is a moving target, effective black infrastructure-building must have specific goals, targets and sustainability plans. Naming racists will be a big business. There is much information to be gleaned about it and information is power and power is money.

This lucrative racist-naming business should be transparent to the black community, it should enrich the biggest risk-takers the most – we are a capitalist society, after all – and put reasonable amounts of money in the pockets of supporters. Success means having multiple leaders step up to incorporate the best-of-the-best ideas going forward.

The following chapters will offer up the most important steps and lessons from the decades-long study of the author on racism and our interaction with it. It is one man's exhaustive research of the problem and its remedies. It is a structure. But, as Luther Vandross sang, "a house is not a home." Take this structure and upgrade it with the minds, wills and talents of 100,000, a million or 10 million black people and it becomes something awesome.

The structure is meant for you, there in North Carolina, to take one or more strategies and make them real. Bring in families and friends. Argue. Fix them. Fail. Start over. Partner with black people in Iowa and New York and make these ideas grow and come alive.

It then becomes as powerful as the Declaration of Independence or the Magna Carta, two documents famous for freeing oppressed people.

Most chapters will deal with single issues, a few will lump issues together. All of them are jumping-off points that are meant to be deconstructed, built up or added to. Use websites, phone calls, meetings or sheets of paper (to avoid the NSA), but imbue these ideas with your own particular brand of survivor genius and the advancement of our community will be stunning. Be brave enough to claim the birthright denied you by the Sons of the South and you will, literally, create a new and better America.

Waging a successful campaign in Civil War IV means there are no permanent allies, only permanent interests. Our collective interest should be in protecting our families and others who look like our families from being blocked from better education, housing, jobs and societal power.

Race is not a ball and chain when it comes to the black community, people can slip out of blackness if they desire. Supreme Court Justice Clarence Thomas has proven time and again he wants nothing to do with black people and our issues. He is free to believe and act as he wishes, but he is bolstering a system that has already proven excellent at denying black people participation.

Race is a commonality. Though many of us have escaped financial hell and some of us are getting by just fine, obstacles still remain, predicated on our skin color. You can choose to ignore that and hope for the best or actively change the script.

It's not surprising if most decide to do nothing. Apathy is a part of human nature and centuries of indoctrination into an inferiority mindset have taught some of us that helplessness is the go-to response. In fact, it's been said many times that black organizations don't work well – NAACP and Urban League jokes abound.

But, organizations are how groups of people change the world for their betterment. The United States is an "organization." Its armed forces are "organizations."

Some black people retain slavery era programming in their heads and that blocks belief in collective black power. It's an odd belief, since groups like Mothers Against Drunk Driving, the National Organization of Women, the Teamsters and thousands of other *organizations* have changed life for the better for white people.

Hell, the Ku Klux Klan is an organization that wants to fight *individual* black people, not black groups. Why do you think that is?

Bike riders, pregnant women, tall people, geniuses, female executives, gays, environmentalists – all of them band together for their greater good, their common interest. But, when we band together, there is derision from within and without: 'Why do we need a Congressional Black Caucus?' complain certain white people. 'The Congressional Black Caucus is a joke,' complain certain black people.

Race doesn't have to define us or limit us, but it should bring us together to fight obvious injustices to all of us. The former child actor Raven-Symone exemplifies the old way of thinking that blackness must be denied to get ahead. She very publicly declared herself as "not African American" and, since she was involved in relationships with women, she decided to add she's "not a lesbian" either. That is a stance for which the Sons of the South pray. Each black person who disavows blackness supports white supremacy by default.

The Habit of Blackness

Black people have to hang onto the habit of blackness, something too few truly value. Given a choice to identify as black, golfer Tiger Woods invented a word, 'Cablinasian,' rather than accept the fact of his blackness.

That's his choice. Still, the habit of blackness allows us to take advantage of what we have earned by blood: citizenship, a rung on the economic ladder, great population numbers, understanding of white people, money, land, skills and so much more.

It requires full-time and concerted oppression to keep such a talented people down. In the words of Public Enemy, it takes a nation of millions to hold us back - unless we remain complicit in our own oppression.

Then, when injustice is defeated, we can define ourselves for a new era. And, shame on the community that defers fighting the good fight so the next generation can do it.

It is now 400 years since North American slavery's inception. The enemy's strategy has become obvious and the warmongers are lazy with repeated victories. We, the descendants of the world's mightiest survivors, have an opportunity to not only end the war, but to win it. We have the power to provide our own salvation.

Life and art are sprinkled with salvation. A billion tales of hopelessness have been fixed by the simple acts of looking around – that is the central theme of biblical Abraham on Mt. Moriah. In the modern world, the newly poor find million-dollar copies of Action Comics #1 in the walls of the home they are about to lose. Homeless men are accidentally given diamond engagement rings, do the honest thing, return it and are gifted with a hundred thousand dollars, factory workers walk dozens of miles to work and back each day, are noticed and rewarded for their struggles with cars and cash.

It's luck, but it works for societies, too. The Pilgrims were "lucky" that a plague had killed off 90 percent of the New World's native population prior to their arrival, allowing them easier battles by which to take their lands.

The operative word is 'work.' We've got to put in the work. The harder we work, the luckier we'll get.

We can disagree; we can re-sculpt the forms of the strategies suggested by this book, but above all else, we must act.

Act with urgency. Have a phone number, email, text address or a living, breathing person to talk to. Tell them, 'You and I are going to make this happen.' Then, make it happen. The Civil Rights Movement started with a phone call that sounded like every other in the black community: "I'm tired of this shit …"

The only difference was somebody said they were going to change it and followed through. That's it. It's the extent of the magic. A decision to act was followed by a true action. That is the recipe for the Manhattan Project, the lunar landing, America.

Two steps: Deciding. Acting. And, a third, important, step for the black community is to report back. Give honest accounts of progress and failures. Talk to each other.

Futurist Alvin Toffler said, "You've got to think about the big things while you're doing the small things, so that the small things go in the right direction."

Black people are sophisticated survivors; we understand the truth in that statement. So, while we have been blessed to have the Rosas, Malcolms, Martins, we don't really need giants. We need pragmatic visionaries; we need gifted managers. We can get to where we need to go with the Ann Fudges, Kasi Lemmonses and Lonnie Johnsons.

All that we need ask of them is this: "Don't impersonate a cause. Be with us in this moment and offer us the best you have. There is no need to reinvent the wheel – many people are already doing what needs to be done. Help us manage our existing talents to escape the oppression we endure daily."

These talented managers will help shape how we do what we need to do in order to be ascendant. They may come up with one way or several. They may tweak our organizing or more clearly identify who will try to stop us and how and suggest our best reactions to their opposition.

They will assume the role of author Isaac Asimov's fictional character, Hari Seldon, the star of his 'Foundation' science fiction trilogy.

In Asimov's books, Seldon was the only one to see the existing world order – the Galactic Empire – as unsustainable. The Empire was oppressive, corrupt and spiritually bankrupt. Sound familiar?

Seldon invented a discipline called psychohistory, which could make accurate predictions of mass societal behavior and he calculated the Empire was dying. Not just that. After it died, there would be 10,000 years of cruelty and war unless it could be replaced by some other form of galactic government.

Seldon came up with the Foundation, which would shrink that 10,000 year period down to 1,000 years. That is our task – to come up with something better in a shorter time than would happen without our intervention.

Black revolutionaries in the 1960s spoke of a concept called the '10,000 Year Pageant. It suggests black people go through dormancy and ascendancy in 10,000 year cycles. They may be right. We may be ready to party like it's 9999.

Chapter 2
The Database:
Track Your Enemies and Hold Them Accountable

Dream all you want/'Cause all the light you occupy/They will try/ and take it all from you - **'I Had No Right,' PM Dawn**

One of the most absurd statements white people make is that racism is over. They repeat it over and over and over. You probably heard it a few minutes ago.

Malcolm X would slap his forehead, dumbfounded, if he were alive today.

Pick your reply; any of them are logical enough to refute that silliness: If racism is dead, why are there more KKK groups than there have been since the 1950s? If racism is dead, why do we see Donald Sterling and Nevada Welfare Queen Cliven Bundy making news?

If racism is dead, why are black drug users 20 times more likely to be arrested for drug offenses compared to white drug users? If racism is dead, why do black men receive 20 percent more jail time for the same crimes as white men? If racism is dead, why is black net worth five percent of white net worth? If racism is dead, why are there only two black CEOs of multibillion dollar companies?

It's shooting fish in a barrel. But, they are very indifferent fish because, no matter how much logic you use to blast away the lies, the people who say this have already made up their minds. Their ignorance has calcified.

So, here's what black people need to understand. White people really don't see race unless black is involved. But, don't misunderstand – that's not racial colorblindness, nor is it a good thing. In the absence of black people, the concept of white splinters into hatred against other whites – Jews, Irish, Germans, Italians.

And, even supporters of racial fairness have a "movie of the week" attention span. They support the latest, sleekest cause, be it gay marriage, immigration or global warming. It's not precisely correct to call them fair weather supporters, but compared to the white people who loathe black people, they are inconstant.

It's reasonable to assume that very conservative white people don't even like other white people if they're not related. So, if they don't like non-familial white people, what chance do black people – who possess a higher degree of 'otherness' in their eyes – have for fair play? Is it racism or misogyny? Probably a combination of both, but the main fact remains that slavery's 500-year-old marketing campaign is alive and well.

Race is not behavior; it is an observable reality of human differences, just like hair or eye color or height. But, the slave trade made it something more. Because the Atlantic slave trade dealt with people of different colors, it made it easy to differentiate slave from slaver. In early history, white people enslaved white and black people enslaved black. The reason? They were the closest.

Once transportation techniques had evolved enough to allow humans to crawl across the globe, things never before witnessed in the world began to happen.

One of them was the rescue of Europe by Africa. Sub-Saharan and North Africa – Egypt is part of Africa – possessed thriving civilizations and technologies; there was higher math, advanced architecture and farming. More importantly, its people weren't dying from the Black Plague. Europe lost nearly 60 percent of its population in seven years, between 1346 and 1353, when the plague raged through it. Most of those deaths were slaves or serfs. Those slaves were the economic engine of a pre-industrial age.

Until that time, the races really were mostly separate and equal. When black or white adventurers showed up on distant shores, human motives were ascribed to each others' actions and those adventurous people, black and white, mixed freely.

But, slavery's central evil was one of visual differentiation suggesting inferior or superior humanity. Africa "gifted" Europe with masses of people of another color and Europe returned the favor by destabilizing Africa for the next 600 years.

Dark-skinned slaves were instantly identifiable. They had no ability to blend in. Because they were from another culture, they were hobbled by language from engaging in verbal arguments for freedom.

Europe compounded its evil by deciding to label these fellow human beings as subhuman. As late as 1866 – after the end of U.S. Civil War I – the Holy Office of Pope Pius IX affirmed that it was not against divine law for a slave to be sold, bought or exchanged.

He literally blessed the slave trade: declaring enslaved Africans as soulless creatures undeserving of freedom by the will of God.

As millions of people were bled off from their mother land's shores, Africa lost its future. Brilliant doctors, builders, technicians, generals, educators, mathematicians, geniuses and leaders never achieved their potentials because they were either enslaved or murdered. Europe and the Americas grew strong with a trillion hours of free labor, while Africa stagnated.

More than a half-millennium of marketing strategy was aimed at making white people and black people believe black people are inferior. Logic and science are hard pressed to make a dent in this ignorance-by-design. Still, inroads have been made. It's been slow, but that speed must be measured against 500 years of global slavery compared to only 50 years that have been truly committed to equality.

And, the hard-won treasure of the Civil Rights Movement was a pedestrian equality that meant black people could no longer be lynched or otherwise murdered for no good reason, had to be paid wages for their work and possessed the same rights as other Americans.

But, the Sons of the South have been busy working behind the scenes to erode that equality – black people can no longer be lynched for no good reason, but they can be killed if they are even thought to be a threat, as Trayvon Martin's murderer knows. That man received $200,000 from internet well-wishers for killing an unarmed teen. Black people must be paid for their work, but they can still be denied work and even if they do find employment, the wages don't have to be livable. And, as far as rights – that is America's biggest bait and switch. The rights of drug-abusing radio host Rush Limbaugh are far broader and more accommodating than those of Joe Sixpack. You have rights if you have money or white skin – in that order.

Yet, there are white people, blind to the hypocrisies of anti-government Tea Partiers on the dole, who wonder why black people complain about their lot in life.

It is the black person's burden. They continually battle benighted white people who accept the lies of black genetic inferiority; educate well-meaning white people who earnestly believe American society offers equal opportunities and discard black people who struggle against our future.

In a war like Civil War IV, you can't save everyone. Some people have to be viewed as lost causes. Just as a few Jews supported the Nazis and a few black people owned slaves, some people have internalized the lies.

The only strategy that works for those lost souls is to keep track of them and then cast them out to minimize the harm they cause.

Jews have proven particularly adept at this. After the horrors of World War II, they collectively vowed, 'Never again. A better, black-themed vow would be, "No more."

Jews became "Nazi Hunters" – even into the 21st century chasing brittle, ancient men. They created anti-defamation leagues. They researched histories, published names; pointed fingers at individuals and organizations. They collected figurative GPS data on every anti-Semite they could find so they might lessen the negative impact on their community by either keeping those people away or going after them.

We can and should create a similar mechanism. In a nation of 200 million white people, it is amazing that we have, maybe, 13 self-proclaimed racists.

A wise person doesn't take her adversary's word that he doesn't wish her harm and, luckily, in this era of electronic communication, she doesn't have to.

Step 1 in manufacturing a better future for black people is this: create "The Database."

With modern computing power, millions or even billions of datapoints are no longer difficult to manipulate. We see that power everyday in our credit card transactions, both online and at point of purchase. It is startlingly easy to create a centralized, black-owned and -operated database that tracks each and every racist behavior perpetrated on any of America's 45 million black citizens.

Whether you live in Quincy, IL and are denied a job because of your race, or are called a nigger by a cop in Brooklyn, NY, it all goes into one place and any authorized black person may contribute to it – just like Wikipedia – or search its database – just like Google.

When we input information by computer or phone in the identities of those who hate us, most will no longer be cloaked in darkness. Even better, we can act on the information – boycott businesses, call for police officer resignations, investigations and more.

Because we are a fair and just people, this database will require some failsafe measures. We must ensure we get the haters' correct identities – badge numbers are great identifiers; we must allow other black people, who disagree, to input data on behalf of the accused white person and we must have regular updates. If a white person

44

has truly repented, being labeled an official racist shouldn't be a social death sentence.

The idea is simple. Give each white person who interacts with black people a 'Racist Rating." A high rating – say, a '10' – indicates he hates black people and should be either avoided or confronted, depending on the circumstances. A low rating – 0 or 1 – would mean the person is fair-minded and thoughtful in regards to race.

Then, we are able to break racisms down to their constituent components. Rape, murder, physical assault and economic violence – job, housing and loan discrimination – generate the most negative scores. Verbal and written abuses constitute a lower level.

White people who refuse to interact with black people would be analogous to people who have no credit rating. They'd be ciphers who, for better or worse, are mistrusted by the community until they define themselves.

A great side effect is The Database will point to those pulling the strings of racial hatred; it will definitively identify the Sons of the South and prevent them from doing their dirty deeds in the dark.

Racist ratings take into account the reality of power; it fits the *racisms* model of the 21st century. White crackpots may receive damning, but relatively low-impact, racist ratings because they call people, 'nigger.' But, law enforcement officers, judges, politicians, landlords, employers would fare the worst because their ratings are based on systemic abuses of power.

Done properly, the ratings will lead directly to action and call into question the hiring and employment of racists. A police department that knowingly hires or promotes racists would be damning itself.

It will expose the top levels of all organizations; fostering questions such as, "Does Mark Zuckerberg have any black friends?" Because, he sure doesn't have any black employees.

It's well known that black computer science graduates are much more likely than white computer science graduates to be ignored by the tech sector. So, Facebook is no worse or better than Google or Twitter or Uber or Ebay or Amazon.

Identifying enemies is logical, non-invasive, fair-minded and good policy. As such, it will be attacked aggressively by more than the usual suspects – the conservative white Republican base and their Sons of the South masters.

Simply creating this system demands collective soul-searching from our community. Big questions must be asked and answered honestly.

- Should we collect this information?
- What do we do with the information about who hates?
- Are we prepared to act?
- Who is black?

Those four questions are huge. They speak not only to whether a collective resolve for fairness exists in the current black community, but whether the community will act on what it finds. Guaranteed, it will find racism.

Also guaranteed is that the deepest resistance will be from our own, black-hating black people like Clarence Thomas and GOP operative Ron Christie.

We are not a monolithic people. We are affected, like all humans, by the places of our birth, our families, and our unique lives. Some of us truly don't like black people and others are fine with the status quo. Racism, in their minds, should be left alone.

Southern black people are well-known for their stand on being called 'nigger' by white people: 'I'd rather have someone call me that to my face than behind my back,' many Southerners say. 'That way, I know who I'm dealing with.'

Black people from other regions see it as a sign of disrespect and prefer that racist white people stifle their hate-speak when black people are around.

Still, black Southerners will bristle if you tell them they accept racism. Like most social strategies, there is no one, clear-cut truth. The 'no disrespect' strategy of Northern black people hasn't stopped racism from existing in areas outside of the South.

On the other hand, black Southerners have virtually no statewide political representation in their region. In fact, their states are so solidly Republican that statewide politicians have no problem demonizing black people because 90 percent of white people vote Republican and are vocal in their hatred of Obama.

Sure, there are a very few federally elected officials from predominantly black districts, but for a region with the majority of America's black population, it is a travesty how little representation they have at the state level. And, make no mistake, the state level controls the local level – ask the predominantly black cities of St. Louis and Detroit.

Still, the black Southern strategy of knowing one's enemy is smart. Where it fails miserably is with follow-through. Klansmen, Confederate traitors, Tea Partiers, Obama Secessionists and Nazis walk unaccosted down Southern streets because they fear no repercussions from black Southerners.

Any strategy of identification is absurd without subsequent action. The Civil Rights Movement would have been a historical footnote if its leaders had simply identified city bus policies as discriminatory.

Their action was to boycott. Action empowered their identification.

Southerners know who the racists are, but their actions have no follow through. Creating a national database can and must lead to action. Racists will hate it – as well as a lot of black people.

Why? Because, it will mean taking a stand. It will mean rocking the boat. Rocking the boat could capsize their tiny financial dinghies.

People fear change because a lifetime of subsistence trains some to think that the only change possible is for the worse. It's not surprising that one of the few people who went on record to say that President Obama should be lynched was a black man. That is the fruit of 500 years of a 'Mad Man'-slick slavery campaign.

Malcolm X, certainly, and Dr. King, probably, had black traitors in their organizations that helped lead to their deaths. The state of Mississippi hired black spies to sabotage civil rights efforts – men and women who fought against their own equal rights. Change is frightening.

So, to combat the critical issue of in-house traitors, a monumental task must be performed.

We need to redefine blackness for the 21st century.

In 500 years of slavery and 239 years in America, we have *never* been allowed to freely choose blackness, it was forced on us. The one-drop rule, the brown paper bag tests, slavery, Jim Crow, all of these strategies defined blackness for us. Our contribution was simply to keep on living as black people. It wasn't until the 1970s that we could even suggest a name – African American – for our existence.

It is no wonder that light-skinned black people 'passed' back in the 19th and 20th centuries and never looked back. It is also no wonder that when the US Census first offered check-boxes for race that included 'multiracial,' a million black people disappeared overnight. 'Black' had endured centuries of bad-mouthing, so none of this is surprising to anyone living in black skin.

Tiger Woods chooses not to be black. And, who can blame people like him? He doesn't look white, but when given the choice, that's where his allegiance lies. Millions of dark-skinned, African-descended Americans feel the same as Tiger.

In the enlightened 21st century, black people still struggle to feed, shelter and clothe their families at a magnitude of difficulty about 20 times greater than their white peers. Much like their enslaved forebears, most have nothing left to give to their children at the end of their lives, while white children are bequeathed homes, businesses, jobs and passes to the front of the economic line.

The most apparent path out of destitution – professional sports – is a lottery win. Besides needing the physical talents and thousands of hours of practice time, potential pro athletes are required to deal with politics and extremely limited space on rosters. The great 20th century basketball player, Julius "Dr. J" Erving, once remarked that there were dozens of guys he played against on playgrounds that had pro-level talent. But, major professional sports teams cater to white audiences. Having too many black players is considered a hard sell.

So, is it coincidence when the number of African Americans in major league baseball drops to historically low levels? Is it further coincidence that the NBA – America's blackest sports league – has seen its percentage of black players drop in favor of predominantly white foreign players?

The music industry was on the same trajectory as sports; it is common knowledge, for instance, that early MTV outright refused to play music by black artists. Michael Jackson made some inroads, but the wall was truly torn down by a vibrant new music and community that young black kids created in our inner cities.

Until hip hop became a multi-billion dollar industry capable of wildly enriching white music executives, the black community was an orchard from which white America picked and chose. The Beatles liked 'Twist and Shout,' so they took it. Elvis Presley sounded kinda black, so he claimed R&B.

But, hip hop – born as both a music and community – would not be appropriated so easily. When white rapper Eminem rose to the top of the musical heap, he couldn't be separated from the culture of the music. He was surrounded by black faces and steeped in black inner-city mores.

Hip hop was indivisible, one of the most powerful modern expressions of the depth of black culture. It had grown separate and apart but, mostly, it had grown strong despite the privations demanded by white society. And, that's just black *youth* culture.

Most Americans still don't desire to be black. But, the wonderful experiences of black culture are at least being appreciated by some.

For those of us descended from Africans, right now is the time to decide to be black – or not. The Database demands it. Its process only works if a large group of people decide to identify and act on racist behaviors. That can't happen without the large group being unified.

It is similar to Obamacare in that it requires a critical mass of members to declare they will participate. Otherwise it is vulnerable to social hacking: black people who oppose it would be able to sabotage it with false input; white people could join and gum it up the process by fighting charges of racism.

No, the only way for The Database to function properly is for its first three rules to be:

- Users must identify as black
- Users must be who they say they are and
- Users must be in support of identification of racists and subsequent action.

Those three rules are the only ones that give it a chance.

The Database is a logical continuation of our Jewish-Mexican model of community building. Like the famed Nazi hunters, it puts misdeeds in the public eye – not just in the realm of boogeyman tales for little black children.

Creating it could be as easy as designing a website and putting it on the internet for the world to see.

It won't be that easy.

The first hurdle will be what our parents called the 'Crabs in a barrel' problem. Our best and brightest will trip and trample competitors in order to found The Database and make the money that can be made. Our collectively limited circumstances have created a million-person line of smart, ambitious entrepreneurs who have had 100 million chances snatched away from them because of race, timing, lack of cash, etc. Some of us are financially stable and hungry for fame and greater fortune; others are literally hungry.

This is the curse and blessing of capitalism; competition is fierce and dirty. More than one group will want to make this happen.

Though the process will still work if 18 Databases pop up from Bangor to Las Vegas, it will be slowed down. Consider: competition is meant to sharpen the offering so the consumer gets what he or she wants. But in-the-market competition takes time to anoint winners and losers. Eighteen competing Databases would generate bad feelings between competitors, business espionage, price wars and negative outcomes for the consumer.

It would also feed into the inferiority myth that if black people created it, it isn't any good. Eighteen databases varying in quality and service would fragment the market and the message of unity would be lost. A community service would thus become a cash cow for a select group.

And, even if the 18 companies eventually combine into one high-functioning entity, that evolution is slowed by personalities, demands, in-fighting, misunderstandings – you know, human nature. Time will be wasted.

Time is one of those things that the slavery mentality has branded us as incapable of grasping. It is a racist trope from the era when the Sons of the South fought to keep us out of the business community by saying we had no concept of time, money or honor, thus CPT, or colored people's time, was born.

In this case, time really isn't on our side.

51

A project this central to changing America's racist habits can't languish. It doesn't have the luxury of false starts and do-overs. Whichever group takes the lead on creating The Database will have the resolve of each and every member tested because white society will try and tear it down with both love and anger.

"Oh, it's a great idea, but…" progressives will say. "It's racist," conservatives will mutter.

But, Martin Robison Delaney said it best. "Every people should be the originators of their own designs, the projector of their own schemes, and creators of the events that lead to their destination – the consummation of their desires."

If there are 'buts' to The Database, we can easily resolve them and if white people consider it racist to identify racists, that speaks more to their issues than ours.

The first step is to have an honest, nationwide dialog on who has the best chance of making The Database happen. Then, whoever comes out best, whether they are in Delaware or California, should be supported. Because when the odd credit checks, unexpected background investigations and out-of-place loiterers materialize, it will take the comfort of a solid group of true believers to continue forward.

The Database creative team profile calls for a group that draws on young, fiercely pro-black warriors with the help of technically savvy young to middle-aged business types and old heads with some wealth who grasp the concept if not the technical specifics. Sista Soulja, Issa Rae, Common and Morgan Freeman would be a celebrity team that could make it happen. But, celebrities are not required. The only requirements are belief and perseverance.

The concept is simple – track your haters and hold them accountable. To sign up for The Database you must provide proof you are a black person and sign a declaration that you:
- are not looking to change your race anytime soon
- are who you say you are

- won't cheat the system by using more than one user name
- support the black community
- will only input data for those who you witnessed in person being racist
- will not falsely accuse anyone of racism

Expect Resistance

Since we are the black community – the children of survivor warriors, let's get the bad news out of the way. The list of those who will try to stop The Database will be a mile long because it has the potential to change the balance of power. Remember the scene in the film "X"? The one where Malcolm X has hundreds of members of the Fruit of Islam standing at attention, refusing to depart until he raised his hand and pointed his finger?

A white NYPD cop said nervously, 'No one man should have all that power."

This will be "too much power" in their eyes.

Potential opponents include the FBI, the CIA, the NSA, federal, state and local governments, the ACLU, both national and local Republican Parties, white people of any party aggrieved by being called racist, not to mention actual racist groups who fear black people at best and are terrified of any organized efforts by our community.

The excuses given will also be numerous:
- Invasion of privacy
- Potential for inaccuracy
- Inadequate authority
- Potential for abuse
- Lack of support from the community en toto
- "Black racism"
- No need for it

But, before succumbing to that fog of lies and half-truths, the wise person will consider the context. The NSA at this second is spying on virtually every American; that proves there is no electronic privacy. Read the fine print offered by any tech titan – Google, Yahoo!, Facebook, Apple – they all collect, save and sell your data.

Who gives them that authority? Who ensures they don't abuse it? Who clears up inaccuracies? What community supports them 100 percent?

Most importantly, look at the massive amount of snooping our financial industry has done for years. Did you sign up for a credit rating? A FICO score? No. It's the same thing black people have seen for 400 years – "We are allowed to do this, but you are not. And, if you try, we'll change the rules."

The Database for white people has long existed – without controversy – in multiple forms. Their databases track your credit, your phone calls, your texts, your emails, your shopping patterns, your online searches, your Facebook posts.

The wise person has to ask herself, "Why is it OK for them, but not for me?"

It's the 21st century, white people have moved on to other social causes, gay marriage, global warming, immigration, "leaning in." But, we have never been a cause; we've always been a people living and dying for ourselves and our families. After the "cause" fades in the minds of white people, we endure.

Understand that it is highly unlikely that a community in which 99.9 percent of our fortunes are self-made, a community that produced President Barack Obama, Lonnie Johnson, Bob & Sheila Johnson, Dr. Dre, Michael Jackson, Michael Jordan, Ann Fudge, Kenneth Chenault and millions more, is so defective that we can't overcome myriad permutations of poverty.

Logic suggests there is a systemic issue and, logic be damned, anyone with common sense can see it. One woman can't fight the system. To combat systemic inequities, a rival system must be created. Those who don't see a need for The Database aren't paying attention.

Their resistance, our response

The first and best weapon used will be the old favorite – divide and conquer. It will begin with whispers in the ear that fly onto Facebook pages. "Lamar should be the leader, not Sheri." Or, "I hear Bebe is a drunk, she doesn't need to be involved in this."

The divisions will appear as if they come from within – 'Oh, those crazy black people can't organize anything!' – but there will be very interested parties pulling the strings. They'll use money, sex and secrets for leverage and cheer for a burning house.

The second step will be their go-to, their wrecking ball – government. Some portion of The Database will be dragged into a court of law and the Sons of the South will be in their element. American courts are thoroughly experienced at diminishing the rights of black citizens.

From Affirmative Action to 100-to-1 ratio drug laws to 'Stand Your Ground' to neo-slavery incarceration to limited voting rights to disparate sentencing for the same violations, the courts have proven to be an unapologetic opponent of black people.

The most obvious attack will be trumped-up charges of invasion of privacy, which will give predominantly white privacy advocacy groups cover. To make it personal, the principals who found The Database will be named in lawsuits in an effort to show them who's the boss. It's similar to whipping the first slave nearly to death to make an example for the hundred slaves looking on. Sap their collective will, i.e., terrorize them, and a group will not oppose its oppressor.

The answer is a two-pronged attack. First, sue back. Take their asses to court, be it the federal government or Bob Blow. Judges may hate black people, but they love litigation and the slower the better. The slow pace can work in our favor, allowing The Database to grow more powerful.

Second, take the case to the court of public opinion – so long as it's the opinion of black people. This is part of the reason why supporters must declare themselves early on. The Civil Rights Movement wasn't a panacea, but it did impart some power on the black community. It didn't change the verdict in Simi Valley back in the late 20th century, but you can bet there is the fear of going too far in even the most racist mind. That is a rational fear, since a good portion of California and other states burned in the aftermath of that travesty and an innocent white man was beaten nearly to death.

Simply shutting down a potential tech giant for no good reason – an organization with customers, employees, revenues, and tax payments – is much the same as having a 19th century lynching in 2014. There would be no cover.

So, the solution is to make sure there is no cover. Be as transparent and above board as an incorporated entity can be and cultivate the faith of your customers.

Come up with a catchy name for The Database, blueprint it and use our collective genius to define the many racisms of the 21st century. Quantify racist behavior to the point where a user can just pull down a list of what he experienced and input the identifying information of the racist in a matter of seconds.

If done properly, our allies will grow by the day because we will be doing something good and positive for a community accustomed to wretched treatment.

These actions will lead to something wonderful. Millions of black people will have the luxury of asking, 'What do we want our culture to be in the 21st century?'

We will be forced to look at the internal issues we have perennially placed on the back burner while we tried to put out kitchen fires. We will deal with light versus dark skin, bougie versus street, gay versus straight, rich versus poor and finally resolve the whole 'acting white' thing.

Being black in America is analogous to being served meals in prison. We have no control over the menu, timing, taste or nutritiousness, but it's kept us alive.

Now, that prison sentence is over. The menu is up to us. We are able to define, more fully than at any point in our history, what it means to be black.

No disrespect to the hip hop community, which reflects the good, bad and neutral of our youth culture, but, hip hop is one sliver of an extremely deep culture. We are matriarchal, patriarchal and complex. That complexity has allowed us to survive on fields meant to kill us.

To move forward it's crucial that we identify the chains foisted upon us, issues like drugs and single-parent households, and bluntly question why we continue to let them grow.

All of this may sound like black people will be setting up focus groups and having "very serious" discussions from now until the end of time.

That's the beauty of a fully functioning database such as this. The questions are asked and answered by the code. Defining racism with 1s and 0s uncovers racists and reveals ourselves. For instance, you can't even define being called 'nigger' as racist without some agreement on why it's hurtful. You have to ask who's saying the word. How they're using it, and so on.

That single instance will demand understanding the history of hip hop, social power, lynching, slavery, Jim Crow and a present-day context for comparison.

It will be one of a few thousand such conversations in the evolution of The Database. And, every single conversation will lead to action.

Chapter 3
Our Own Images: Own Our Media

The revolution will be no rerun, brothers/the revolution will be live –
'The Revolution Will Not Be Televised,' Gil Scott-Heron

While The Database goes through its birth pangs, another group of black warriors will need to attack one of the most obvious problems facing black America: the media. That might sound like the rant of a whiny Tea Party member, "Darn media always puts us in a bad light!" The difference is we truly *have* been harmed by the media.

And, the message of American media, despite protestations to the contrary, is that more black representation is a bad thing. Media has reached the end stage of a century-long consolidation. In the 1990s, for example, most Americans got their information from about 15 major media corporations. That number dwindled to six in 2014. Those six are now able to craft any message they desire and chances are many of those messages will be negative toward the black community.

Some of media's historic negativity has been intentional, but now, in the early 21st century, what were once vices are now habits. Black people have been fodder for so long it's hard for white content producers to see us any other way.

The tropes are many and long-lived: Stepin Fetchit, Mammy, Maid, Magic Negro, the starving child, Pimp, Big Scary Black Man, Addict, Watchdog, Noble Martyr.

Studies on the effects of movies and television tell us what we already know – white males are validated by the state of media today. Their senses of self-worth are actually improved through consumption of television, movies, videogames, books, etc.

Over the course of one year, researchers Kristen Harrison and Nicole Martins surveyed about 400 black and white Illinois students. All of the 7- to 12-year-olds were from lower-middle to upper-middle socioeconomic communities.

For white boys, "regardless of what show you're watching ... things in life are pretty good for you," said Martins. "(White males) tend to be in positions of power; you have prestigious occupations, high education, glamorous houses, a beautiful wife, with very (few) portrayals of how hard you worked to get there."

Though it's artifice, media impacts their real world self-esteem. On any given movie night, Little Johnny can see his grown-up self as a superhero, a warrior, a cop, a President, God, a doctor, a genius, a ruler.

No other group is as validated through American media as white males. Even white females are harmed by media-borne sexual objectification.

But, if you ask a white person in the street whether media has any impact on their lives, for instance, 'Does violent television programming lead to violence?' you get shoulder shrugs or outright denials. It's as if the self-esteem that warms the souls of young white men comes from beyond.

'Media doesn't validate these young men,' say the skeptics. 'Its message is neutral.' These people would have you believe a magic signal cuts through the media noise encountered by black people, white women and others who fight oppression on a daily basis and anoints only white males. They have given in to the 'innate superiority of white males' myth.

Let's be clear because, as the great comic Paul Mooney says, it's getting late in the day for bullshit. American media is designed to reinforce the egos of one, and only one, demographic – white males. Because of that, virtually all entertainment and "information" our nation gleans from our media possesses a sympathetic white male viewpoint.

That bias explains circumstances both small and large. The large bias, of course, is the outright banning of black people from the highest positions of power in media. Such inclusion inevitably leads to positive messages for an oppressed people. The Jews are experts at using media to subvert negative messages. We don't yet possess that structure so we are consistently portrayed in a negative fashion.

Smaller biases are legion. For example, black male actors are sexually neutered in most of their fictional roles. Our black men are portrayed as either asexual or chaste. Will Smith, Morgan Freeman and Denzel Washington are three of the biggest movie stars on the planet, but they know their place. Neither Will, Morgan nor Denzel is allowed to kiss any white co-stars. It is rare as hen's teeth for black men to kiss white women in major feature films.

If there is an onscreen romance, Hollywood has to go outside its comfort zone and hire black actresses – which is a great thing! To avoid that, obviously virile leading-man types such as Will, Morgan, Denzel, Wesley Snipes and Eddie Murphy, are paired with Asian, Hispanic or Latina actresses. How many white leading men have been portrayed romantically with black women?

That is one of literally millions of examples of anti-black media behaviors. Rather than feature films with black male and female leads, it avoids those expressions of love, which, of course, would humanize black people to white people. Because America is a media-obsessed nation, we must deal with anti-black messages on a daily basis.

Specific examples include the creation of Fox News, which villainizes most black people; Rush Limbaugh, a drug-addled Missourian with a plantation mentality and a big mouth and insipid magazines like People, US and dozens more that conclude the "Most Beautiful Man/Woman" on Earth is white.

These are just the obvious culprits. There are also "serious" newspapers and magazines with virtually all-white management teams that figuratively parachute into the black neighborhoods of their cities to produce 'woe is me' stories focused on crime and destitution and then ignore the communities for the rest of the year.

"If it bleeds, it leads," goes the old newspaper saying. When it comes to black people, the bloodier the better, it seems.

And, that's just black people in America. Africa, home to a billion human beings, one-seventh of the world's population, is viewed as a continent of dimwitted child kings who rule over people too stupid to find food in paradise.

So, it was extremely unexpected that three generations ago some large media outlets were sympathetic to the plight of the Negro. The raw power of media was demonstrated during those years because the industry led a significant portion of white America away from its entrenched racist behaviors.

The change in racial attitude was so amazing that it's not hyperbole to compare it to changing a person's sexual orientation. It was a monumental achievement and the media knew it.

It transformed a nation of casual racists into a nation which considered racism to be an anti-social behavior. The antics of people like Alabama governor George Wallace were on display for all and picked apart in countless tongue-clucking editorials.

But, for black people, seeing Wallace stand in a schoolhouse doorway shouting, "Segregation now, segregation forever," was considered a quiet Tuesday. Not only was it nothing we'd hadn't seen before, it was gentle compared to the brutality we endured each day.

Black men, women, boys and girls disappeared daily in the South and we weren't allowed to ask questions. Bodies hung from trees as we passed by with our heads lowered and eyes averted. Our meager properties were stolen freely and we had no recourse but to run away.

The problem with our relationship with media during the Civil Rights Movement is we expected a temporary change of heart to become permanent without doing anything to make it happen.

Had Dr. King not been killed, he might have seen the need to form a coalition to purchase CBS. Malcolm X might have led a leveraged buyout of Warner Bros. studios.

Jewish men understood the power of media early. Many of the early founders of motion picture studios were Jewish –Louis B. Mayer, Samuel Goldwyn, William Fox, Jesse L. Lasky, Adolph Zukor, Harry Cohn, Marcus Loew, Harry, Albert, Sam and Jack Warner and Carl Laemmle all attended synagogues.

It is remarkable that they did it at a time of great global anti-Semitism. Through ceaseless and subliminal media insertions, they 'normalized' Jewishness for the masses. Yiddish crept into our national lexicon, actors and actresses who were obviously Jewish were given comedic roles, which graduated to dramatic roles, which over the course of 75 years led to the richest comedic actor in television being Jewish – Jerry Seinfeld. This is the same Seinfeld whose program pictured a New York with hardly any black people in it and whose co-star proved to be a flat-out racist.

Using the Jewish-Mexican strategy is problematic at this point, primarily because Jews have used media to significant social advantage for more than 75 years. That is a hell of a head start. To exactly duplicate their efforts, we would have to form a new media infrastructure upon which most Americans rely. That flies in the face of reality – our media is balkanized. Video games, cable television, YouTube, Instagram, Twitter and more, place us in different camps that don't necessarily subscribe to the same content.

In such a climate, Tyler Perry has done the impossible – he created an entire movie studio with virtually no white help. Many white people hate him for that and some black people hate his message, but his prodigious talent has made him as wealthy as a sultan and, even better, makes him powerful.

Perry has the power to do what our most famous black actors and directors cannot do – have a film reflect exactly what he wants it to reflect. He can "green light" a film and it will happen. Perry is doing what needs to be done, but he is doing it virtually alone. He needs friendly competition and more support.

Esteemed director Spike Lee is to film what the late August Wilson was to the stage. He is a chronicler of the black experience in America. Good, bad and ugly, Lee puts the grandeur of the black experience on film, with no apologies for its pro-black sensibility. That makes the feud between Lee and Perry a 'crabs in a barrel' scenario for their black audience.

Lee accuses Perry of making new age minstrel shows, showing the worst stereotypes of black people imaginable. In this case, Lee is wrong, but right-minded. His message would be better served in a private conversation with Perry because we desperately need Perry's success to multiply and expand to Lee, directors Antoine Fuqua, Lee Daniels and Bill Duke, Oprah and beyond. There are six major movie studios. Each is worth billions. If buying one of them isn't an option, we must create our own in a hurry.

With a population of 45 million people, it is entirely reasonable for black America to have at least three dedicated major film studios, with five being the preferred number.

Our stories have been mangled horribly because of the requirement that they speak to a white male perspective. That mandate has created a century of insanity on film. Who in their right mind can sit through 'Mississippi Burning' and not feel confused that the horrors of the Jim Crow South, the tortures, beatings, disappearances, are seen through the eyes of unaffected white FBI agents? The Civil Rights Movement, according to 'The Help,' 'Driving Miss Daisy' and dozens of other films, was a testament to the rectitude of white people and only incidentally related to the efforts of black people.

That is the misinformation that breaks the will of a people. It's a sturdy message: 'You can't free yourselves unless we help.'

Through media, we are taught helplessness and inferiority. If, by chance, we turn the expectations of the white male perspective on its ear, as Eddie Murphy did in his 1982 buddy cop film, '48 Hours,' then there is a scramble to "fix" that shift. In '48 Hours' Murphy was the obvious star, with veteran actor Nick Nolte in a supporting role. The wheels turned rapidly in Hollywood and another buddy cop movie, 1987's 'Lethal Weapon,' paired Mel Gibson, who is white, with the black straight man – Danny Glover.

Murphy busted a trope to bits. He wasn't the comic relief they expected him to be, he was the star. He created a new kind of hero, a wise-cracking good guy who didn't fear white reprisal. Had '48 Hours' proceeded as the white film studio executives expected, Murphy would have cracked a few jokes, allowed Nolte to save the fictional day and gone on to a solid career as a comic character actor. He would have become a less-offensive 20th century Rochester or Tracy Morgan before Morgan became famous.

But, Murphy's transcendence was a money-maker. The 'Beverly Hills Cop' series made a fortune off the same powerful black man formula and white producers faced a dilemma: movies starring black men could make money, but the messages were empowering for a people they feared empowering.

The blaxploitation films of the 1970s were celluloid examples of those fears. They made money, but the onscreen killing of white people at the hands of black people – black women, even! (You go, Coffey and Cleopatra!) – was too explosive. Plus, turning black actors into stars would give them the power to make hiring demands and soon black camera operators, directors and producers would amass enough power to make substantial changes to the industry.

Blaxploitation was a non-starter at a time when racism still held sway for most of the country.

Blaxploitation died a death of benign neglect. Despite the films being profitable, Hollywood decided it didn't need that kind of money. Which is probably the only time in history that sentence will ever be written.

Hollywood much preferred the stories of Italian mobsters in 'The Godfather' series. These characters were based on the true stories of men who purposely destroyed the black community by pumping drugs into it. That was the kind of anti-hero they could get behind. They consider 'The Godfather' series some of the greatest films ever made. Its virulently racist message is perfectly acceptable to them because it maintained the status quo. The only pain was suffered by black audiences.

Oscar Michaux Nearly Changed Our History

Oscar Michaux was our best bet to share in the power of films. Michaux was a black man who created his own film studio, making 45 films from 1919 to 1948. Like the Jewish founders of Hollywood, he understood implicitly the power of movies, but he also knew the nature of racism. His creation of the Michaux Film and Book Company threw down a gauntlet at a time when his life was forfeit just for appearing "uppity."

Bit by bit, his talent and vision made inroads until, in 1948, his last film, 'Betrayal,' was distributed to theaters serving white as well as black audiences. He made history as the first film producer to accomplish that feat.

He is Tyler Perry's spiritual twin.

'Betrayal' was the last of Michaux' films because he died in 1951. Like many black businesses, there was no solid succession plan. Michaux' kin and friends were too busy with their own struggles to run a movie studio.

Undoubtedly, someone saw the company's potential and tried to run with it. But, with no chance for capital investment and the very real prospect of the business being legally stolen by a white man or burned down in spite, there was too much uncertainty for a people who were forced into the roles of maids and porters to survive.

The Michaux Film and Book Company died with Oscar Michaux and the lost possibilities boggle the mind. If the MFBC had survived into the 21st century, it might be the company producing the billion-dollar Spider-Man film series, with Spider-Man's alter ego being Miles Morales, a black teenager.

Michaux would be mentioned in the same breath as Goldwyns, Zukors and Warners. His heirs would be free to do their own amazing things. The heirs of these three film families, alone, are collectively in possession of more than a billion dollars in wealth.

By contrast, Michaux' heirs are probably struggling financially. Not much is known about them. He married Orlean McCracken and endured a stormy marriage. She gave birth while he was away on business, emptied their bank accounts and ran away with their child. Her father sold Michaux's property and took the money from the sale.

It's reported that Michaux' wife was so certain that white people were going to shut down his business that she felt she had no choice but to leave him for her own economic safety.

This kind of injustice makes hearing some people blame black people for their own economic problems even more infuriating. Much of the 21st century's wealth – not just millionaires and billionaires, but the middle class, too – has 19th and 20th century roots.

The black community will suffer at the hands of systemic racism until they accept these realities. Each generation believes less and less that racism will affect them. This leaves them unprepared to deal with a system that they will fight as individuals – and mostly fail in their efforts.

We do our young no favors by simply telling them racial 'ghost stories' instead of building solutions for their future. Our continuing failure and that of our ancestors is not putting a comprehensive system in place that will battle for them when they can't fight for themselves.

That is not the mission of the Urban League, the NAACP, the Black Panthers. It is the mission of black Microsofts, black Apples, black Fox News.

In a capitalist society, business turns the wheels of progress. Media, medical and technology businesses are ascendant. Our owning a handful of small studios won't budge the wheel enough. We need something bigger to fight bigger.

We need to build movie studios, television studios, radio networks, internet portals, videogame makers, social media platforms, print companies. We then need to be fiercely protective of these businesses. They should court our support by giving us high quality entertainment and information and we should be their solid supporters.

Fox News wins its ratings wars because it tells old white people that brown-skinned folks are the devil. It even hires some brown-skinned folks like actress Stacey Dash to give those white folks the message, personally.

Fox News proves what doesn't need proving – racism is comfortable with lies. The advantage our media would have is that we can sell the truth. The truth is black people are talented in myriad ways. Racism has toughened us. All of our billionaires are self-made. Not one of them received a million dollars from his or her father as a teen-ager, as Bill Gates did. We don't turn a million dollars into a billion dollars. We turn 15 cents into a billion dollars because we have no other choice.

So, in the process of creating new media, we are tasked with taking that Oprah-level individual talent and collectivizing it. There is no other way. The Database can be created by a small group and easily offered up to our masses. A videogame company or a movie studio is an enormous investment of capital and creators and users must work together for it to succeed. We must provide an audience for the creators and allow them to hone their craft. That will be difficult because entertainment is rampant in America.

Combining social good and great entertainment has long been abandoned by Hollywood studios and videogame makers. Videogame makers are perfectly fine with purveying the latest, greatest racism: evil characters are dark-skinned, black men are violent or, simply non-existent in their virtual worlds. White teenagers are learning old lessons in a new book.

We need a collective resolve to support our new media. The wait will be worth it. Think about it. Black actresses will become love interests, heroines of their own stories. They will be seen as beautiful. Standards of beauty will expand enormously, so much so that future NBA players will routinely take dark-skinned women as wives.

That last sentence was facetious, but the fact is that metrics of beauty have been set by the media for generations. And, because American media has a white male default setting, that beauty standard is white female.

There's no reason for that – the only reason a thin-tipped nose is desired more by white males is because most white women have thin noses. The same applies for thin lips. No one is denigrating interracial love; it is perfectly fine. But, give the sisters a fair chance. America is programmed to desire white women.

Programming the Beauty of Black of Women
There is an antidote to that programming: a simple video of a thousand beautiful black women of all shades – or one shade – that parents would require young black men to watch daily.

The faces would quickly fly by with accompanying words and music, almost subliminally. That'd be the homework parents would assign to keep their sons grounded in black beauty at a time of exclusively white beauty standards. Experts call it counter-programming. Our young men would see a thousand beautiful female faces to offset the thousand white female faces they already see daily.

That's a strategy that doesn't require anything more than one person with computer skills, a few thousand pictures of beautiful black women that are paired with music and voice and a desire to even the odds. It can be streamed, put on disk, serve as a 24-hour-channel. It all works.

Another small-group strategy is to create a black-focused media-rating strategy. The NAACP and its Hollywood chapter have already attempted something similar, but it's been overshadowed by GLAAD's gay media rating. It's hardly surprising that there is greater acceptance of gay-friendly ratings because, for the most part, the LGBT community operates with the usual white default. Its core issues of marriage, familial rights and general acceptance are rounding errors of the black struggle.

They fight for acceptance. The black struggle is for survival.

More power to their struggle, because they have appropriated the language and tactics of the Civil Rights Movement and adapted them to the 21st century. But, black America isn't in a position to appropriate the tactics of the gay community because we don't have the capacity to hide in straight, white society. We are not their sons and daughters.

The gay struggle has used its white privilege to its advantage and taken its own page from the Jewish community. Hollywood has a healthy relationship with Jewish people. Jews sit in the seats of power and shape the opinions of the hoi polloi. Gay people have done much the same thing.

Acceptance of gays has been directly proportional to their exposure in mass media. You know the names and programs: Glee, Ellen DeGeneres, Rosie O'Donnell, 'Will & Grace,' 'Modern Family,' Rock Hudson, Elton John, Bryan Singer, Tim Cook.

They've amassed power, told their stories and changed America – for white, gay people.

Except for Tyler Perry and Oprah, we have no such clout. And, only Perry focuses on our stories.

Our biggest, hairiest, most audacious goal should be to quickly create large movie studios. This is one of several goals in this book that will require a strong collective effort. Tyler Perry is lightning in a bottle – a man who slept in his car, barnstormed with religious-themed stage plays across the country and was never assured of any type of success. There was no Samuel Goldwyn inheritance to break his fall.

It's the all-or-nothing scenario all of our biggest success stories have had to overcome. Like every rapper or professional athlete, generations of familial poverty force us to swing for the fences. We have no money to fall back on, so failure means living under a bridge. It's the essence of capitalism, but we have never been offered capitalism. We have always been subjected to capitalist paternalism. We were supposed to survive at the will and whim of white males. We were supposed to rise to a particular station and no further.

That doesn't work for us. Despite being blocked at every turn, we are like trees growing in Brooklyn, pursuing our dreams against all odds. Creating our own, viable, movie studios with only a black audience in mind is the dream Oscar Michaux died pursuing.

Michaux knew we had to tell our own stories or we would remain enslaved. If we can't play gods, heroes, presidents, geniuses, scientists and saviors on our own terms – kissing or killing whom we please – then we are just players on stage; following directions.

To make our studios quickly, it will be necessary to borrow a page from old Hollywood. The studios were competitors, yes, but they were in an industry so unique they could cooperate on certain things. If a movie star was being difficult for one studio, others would blackball her. They were the only game in town and they knew it.

For our new studios, that translates into working together for early industry survival, while carving out strong identities.

Instead of each studio buying their own expensive cameras, they might jointly purchase equipment until each can afford their own. Shared market research, distribution and technology lower the bar for entry.

Most importantly, it should be understood that the primary audience is the 50 million black people who will exist at the time of the new studio's creation. It will be necessary to recalibrate from Hollywood's craziness. Hundred-million-dollar budgets won't be necessary.

The real value will be creating stories that don't currently exist but have been waiting to be told for 400 years. In today's Hollywood, creativity is for white stories. No black 'Memento's or 'Natural Born Killers' or 'Blue Velvets' allowed.

Our sanctioned contributions of inner-city horrors and laughter are profitable and easily ghettoized. But, we have so many more stories to tell, if we take it upon ourselves to take the power to tell them.

Power is never going to be handed to us by Hollywood. The money is too good and too intoxicating. Don't fool yourself for one instant by thinking that Hollywood didn't pat itself on the back for the election of President Obama. Some gave money, sure. But, they congratulate themselves more for their depiction of black presidents on TV and in movies that made white people comfortable with a black man in charge.

When the moneyed groups of black people who take up the call to create these studios begin their difficult task, it will be important for them to understand they are creating a new future where a quarter of black boys and girls study and work in science and technology; where black presidents of both genders are commonplace; where the richest person – not black person, the richest person – in the U.S. is black; where a traffic stop is an irritant, not a death sentence and where mothers and fathers bequeath futures to their children instead of debts and doubt.

That's what an empowered black community can do. Black media alone can't do it; success also requires gargantuan legal and financial parallels. Still, without black media, it's not possible.

Expect Resistance

This is a much larger task than The Database. It will require money, expertise and a sophisticated strategy. Like all of the strategies outlined in this book, it will require our collective wisdom, but this will be one of three strategies – legal and financial systems being the other two – that require the most input.

The most obvious resistance will be from existing Hollywood TV and movie studios. They will want to buy (like BET) or destroy (Michaux Book & Film Company) the new studios, with their preference being destruction. The first salvos will be from their media critics; they will denigrate the quality of the enterprises in paternal fashion. Read a white reviewer's critique of any Tyler Perry film and you'll know the template.

Poking holes in quality is low-hanging fruit for any talent-based industry. But, remember, Kanye West didn't start his career with 'My Dark, Twisted Fantasy' anymore than Prince started his with "Purple Rain" or Michael Jackson debuted with 'Thriller.'

Courage is required. Not creating masterpieces the first time out can be forgiven, but not starting the process because "it's too hard" is unforgivable. President Franklin D. Roosevelt observed, "One thing is sure. We have to do something. We have to do the best we know how at the moment... If it doesn't turn out right, we can modify it as we go along."

American entertainment hit its pinnacles through trial and error. Music, movies, television, comedy, journalism – all rely on finding the sweet spots of both audiences and creators.

The existing media power structure knows it's easier to knock over a pile of bricks than a building. Critics will call early efforts "amateurish," "derivative" and "unnecessary" in hopes of demoralizing the talent behind the projects. What they will fail to realize is that they won't be talking to their usual audience. Their critical services won't be required, because this is something they've never before seen.

That realization will set in and then the big guns will fire: threats, lawsuits, espionage, sabotage of projects, leaks to their media, attempts to block distribution. Some supporters of the New Studios will be demoted in their positions in white media; they'll be harassed or fired.

Some black people will join the naysayers. Because they are black people against black ownership of media giants, Fox News will dash them into their studios and pay them large sums to, 'Say it again – in front of the cameras.'

Existing black media, which ideally should mentor the newcomers, might simply see competition and do their best to do damage.

And, that's just Hollywood and the news industry.

Expect the government and organized crime to want a piece of the action. Both will demand tributes, payoffs, contributions and concessions.

'This is too radical,' they'll say. 'It's communism, not capitalism!'

The IRS will look closely at the New Studios' finances and administration. Mobsters will try to intimidate individuals.

Their Resistance, Our Response

The New Studios strategy will require an army of lawyers to maintain. The audience should be engaged almost daily through our social media efforts – not Facebook, we need "Usbook."

Our one-percenter talents have to take the lead on this and work out threat matrices that will anticipate as many negative scenarios as possible. They will have to create business plans that are as detailed as nuclear bomb blueprints. They will need thicker skins than they have ever had in their lives.

They will need to believe they are working on behalf of generations of black youngsters that don't yet exist.

Our New Studio creators will be like Noah in the Bible – leaders to the next, better place.

If a mantra is needed, it is: "Trust no one but your audience.'

But, that's only half the equation. You, there in New Rochelle, NY and you, out in Compton, CA you need to heed their calls for support. If you don't have the dollars to invest, give some of your time. Listen to their news broadcasts, watch their programming. Buy tickets and tell friends.

Specifically, give them half a decade, five years, to find their storytelling stride. That's the compromise that must be made by both the audience and the talent. Five years is much too short a time to really create a pipeline of great stories. Conversely, it is way too much time for today's American audience to stick around and watch an industry improve.

But, without that compromise, there is a strong chance that we will never own media that sets the tone and tenor of America and the world. Media can't exist without audiences; without an audience, there is no money. Like politics, media sucks planet-sized stacks of cash into a black hole.

The white-owned studios will certainly offer stiff resistance. Without a dedicated black audience, advertisers will find it too easy to starve the enterprise.

In this scenario, you are the "non-believer" in Kanye West's 'No Church in the Wild equation: "What's a mob to a king? What's a king to a god? What's a god to a non-believer, who don't believe in anything?"

Your belief will set the stage for a world-changing success, if you let it.

When it all comes together, the world will see something new. Stories about black people will sound, look and end differently. History will be fuller, more exciting because it won't pretend millions of people don't exist. 'Hood pictures will be part of a larger story that will include black heroines, black anti-heroes and dramas that feature skin color only incidentally.

'We shall overcome,' will fade away as it gives ground to 'We are here.'

Failure can't be an option, because needing permission to tell one's own stories is a remnant of slavery that must be eradicated. Waiting for white people to 'green light' the stories of black people is a sickness that has a very obvious cure.

Chapter 4
Get Our Finances in Order

I'm not a businessman, I'm a business, man!/Let me handle my business, damn! –
'Diamonds from Sierra Leone,' Kanye West, ft. Jay-Z

There is an obvious fact that we black Americans should never forget, though we often do: trillions of dollars – not billions – *trillions* of dollars were stolen from our ancestors and from us. That's not including the trillions of dollars stolen away by slavery. We are an empathetic people, so we focus on the lives of men, women and children who were destroyed by that hateful institution, not the lost dollars.

But, the depiction of slavery as the sole cause of black economic issues and some inherent inability of black people to keep pace has always been a two-pronged, bold-faced lie. When a white person, in person or online, starts to fix their mouths to say, "I never owned a slave…" stop them in their tracks.

Slavery was just the beginning. Its reach was felt into the 2000s when the 'War on Drugs' still imprisoned thousands of black men and women; into the 1990s when the tech bubble excluded black entrepreneurs; into the 1980s when mortgage lending was still being redlined by government fiat. Ask them if they were alive in any of those decades.

This is a chapter about our financial uprising. Pay attention, because aside from the outright murders of our friends, relatives and ancestors, this has been the most shameful behavior of those Sons and Daughters of the South.

With the help of the government – in other words, legally – we have been made subjects of a kleptocracy. Theft has been legalized, so long as it is against us. Stolen wages, homes, careers, ideas, businesses, land, investments has added up to trillions of dollars lost to us.

The reason for that is, again, because we are not allowed to operate under a straight capitalist system, we are forced into capitalist-paternalism. We are not allowed, through force of law, to equally pursue our happiness – 'equal' being the operative word.

Sure, you can buy a home if you are qualified, but chances are you won't qualify, despite having the same income and credit history of a white person. If you do qualify, you will pay tens of thousands of dollars more over the life of your loan.

The Sons of the South have ensured there is no real competition for black finance. Once Acme Bank rubberstamps our rejection, only the predatory are left. All the remaining options are bad and built primarily for black people.

We need a massively parallel system of banking that is ours and ours alone. We need to starve the beast of racial conservatism by opting out of their game of rigged capitalism and kangaroo courts.

After leaving tens of trillions of dollars on the table, we will never catch up playing the same game. It's insanity to expect any kind of economic equalization under these conditions.

Pull back. See the bigger picture of upward mobility that is affected by our financial systems. Upward mobility indicates how much your society values you by the opportunities given. Here's something to ponder: the combined wealth of every black billionaire in America and every black professional athlete in America is a fraction of one white guy's wealth – Warren Buffett. Buffett seems to be a nice guy, still, what if he were a virulent Son of the South? Do you think all his money would have no effect on race relations in America? There are very wealthy people who hate black people and put their money where their mouths are in efforts to make black people struggle.

See the bigger picture by not focusing on what you can do alone. Definitely, try your best and improve your personal circumstances, but if we focus exclusively on individual come-ups we will lose every time because white people are supported by a system that works against us.

Upward mobility studies track whether children are able to surpass their parent's financial standings. For black people, the answer is 'no.' If we don't take power over our circumstances, more than half of black people born into poverty will die in poverty.

In these studies, there are five economic groups bookended by the top 20 percent and the bottom 20 percent. Black children born into poor families rank – as a group – with high school dropouts on upward mobility. Statistically, black children have a three percent chance of moving from lowest- to highest-earning economic level; high school dropouts have a one percent chance.

Being born black means being a high school dropout – in white society – even if one is a college graduate. The studies show that even white felons are hired before qualified black applicants with no criminal records.

We are collectively stranded by the existing financial system.

Use common sense, how do we catch up when we have to pay $1,000 for every $100 white people pay on their loans? That disparity makes a white person a millionaire by the time a black person has paid for half of a small house.

Some portions of finance are complicated, but many more portions are simple. If you want to get ahead, someone has to suffer for your good fortune. All the financial equations in the world can't hide the fact that we and our ancestors were the designated scapegoats and contributed greatly to America's prosperity with little to show for it. Slavery was just the opening act.

Ta-Nehisi Coates' meticulously researched article on reparations in the May 2014 edition of The Atlantic magazine described the financial advantage white Americans have over black Americans. He described it as such a huge divide that "poor black households" was not an accurate enough description. Coates quoted economists calling them "ecologically distinct" – a different species of thing.

Further, the income differentials between black and white in 2014 – despite "slavery being dead" – were the same as in 1970. The needle hadn't moved in 44 years. In fact, according to social scientists interviewed by Coates, black children born into affluent neighborhoods are vastly more likely than their white peers to live in a lower-income neighborhood in their adulthood. That's not because they want to give back to the community, it's because they can't afford to live elsewhere.

Even under supposedly liberal White House administrations, black people were fair game for the Sons of the South.

President Franklin Roosevelt's 'New Deal,' was supposed to help poor Americans, with a central, controversial inclusion being "old age insurance," what we now call Social Security.

But, the law was designed with Southern lawmakers' help to purposely exclude the majority of black Americans by exempting domestics and farm-workers from benefits. According to Coates, about 60 percent of all black people were ineligible and that number soared to about 80 percent in the South.

The same shenanigans happened with the G.I. Bill, which had a Title III section that gave veterans access to low-interest home loans. Veterans Administration offices across the country flat-out refused to grant black veterans their legal due.

Blocking home ownership, the path virtually all white families took to become middle-class, was never incidentally discriminatory. The federal Home Owners' Loan Corporation was very specific in its policies to prevent home ownership by black people.

Coates: 'The American real-estate industry believed segregation to be a moral principle. As late as 1950, the National Association of Real Estate Boards' code of ethics warned that "a Realtor should never be instrumental in introducing into a neighborhood … any race or nationality, or any individuals whose presence will clearly be detrimental to property values." A 1943 brochure specified that such potential undesirables might include madams, bootleggers, gangsters – and "a colored man of means who was giving his children a college education and thought they were entitled to live among whites.'

'The federal government concurred. It was the Home Owners' Loan Corporation, not a private trade association, that pioneered the practice of redlining, selectively granting loans and insisting that any property it insured be covered by a restrictive covenant – a clause in the deed forbidding the sale of the property to anyone other than whites.'

Housing, old age benefits, even family traditions were stolen away from black families. Black farmers were direct descendants of slaves who never turned away from the grueling agricultural industry. Many bought their farms with money saved over the course of generations; others were granted land by former owners who finally saw them as fellow human beings. In either case, every black farmer's land was bought and paid for.

But, the U.S. Department of Agriculture, like the FHA, SSA, VA and other alphabet soup government agencies, sought to destroy the livelihoods of black people. As with housing loans, the Agriculture department gave loans to white farmers, but refused black farmers anything.

Black farmers probably wouldn't have minded, given their independent nature and understanding of racism, but as American's population grew, farming grew more technological to keep up with demands.

The USDA's racism meant no improved tractors, no insurance against bad growing seasons, no pest-resistance seeds and on and on. All of the things that insulated white farmers from failure were denied to black farmers. Black farmers couldn't compete because competition wasn't allowed. They were hijacked so their valuable lands could be foreclosed on. The fruit of generations of blood and sweat was stolen.

But, economic justice is salvageable from this cluster-mess. A massively parallel system can be created, but the collective will required is pretty significant.

Creating a parallel financial system means dropping the banks, credit unions, payday loan stores, giant retailers, mortgage companies, savings and loans and sundry other financial institutions that enrich themselves on black struggle.

At present, there is no alternative to them. The insurance, auto, housing and banking industries have colluded with government to bar entry for most competitors to the field. Founding a bank is a gauntlet of credit checks, background checks, accounting regulations and more.

Those are relics of 19th century thought. The 21st century is more flexible in the ways we manage our finances. Mobile banking, as done by the Commercial Bank of Africa is growing. Online security is strong enough that online spending is nearly as safe as in-person banking.

Importantly, we know that banking is not just money, it's about relationships. Those relationships were rarely ours to enter, but with a black-focused financial system, that would change things.

It would still be in keeping with the Jewish-Mexican strategy. Certainly, there are many banks that are owned or administered by Jews. But, in this case, the Mexican component of the equation takes precedent. Mexican expatriates send their money back to Mexican banks and individuals each year by the billions of U.S. dollars.

Even though they make their homes here, they support the financial institutions of their mother country. It's a matter of national pride to them.

We don't have another country to shore up our egos, America is it for us. Still, we've always been seen as strangers in our home. Mexicans come here, Nigerians come here, Chinese come here and they leave nations that, for better or worse, are run by people who look like them. That is psychologically powerful. It sustains their self-esteem. For instance, there is no real "first Mexican president" milestone. There will certainly be a president of Mexican-descent in the U.S. in the future, but there have been dozens of Mexican presidents in Mexico.

So, when middle-class homeowners and laborers come here from other lands, they see the U.S. financial system as a whitewashed version of the banks they dealt with back home. They don't know about the generations of racial exclusion mandated by both the private sector and governments.

All we have ever seen is Mr. Charlie – and Mr. Charlie doesn't like our kind. Creating a massively parallel system that isn't discriminatory against us has the power to change that dynamic forever. It would be our moon landing.

The present financial system has gotten us to where we are – the year 1970 – when it comes to net worth of black people versus white people. Black businesses are the smallest in size of all demographic groups. Starved for loans that are never coming, they can't grow and so most have no employees other than the owner. Their annual revenues are miniscule next to those of white women, Asians, Native Americans and Hispanics. Black businesses are primed to fail because they have virtually no access to capital.

So, imagine asking for money for your business and receiving it with a minimum of hassle. No more complaints along the lines of, 'That white lady got a loan and her business was worse off than mine.'

Imagine receiving a fair rate that is the same, or lower, than white customers.

That has to be a good feeling to know that you're being judged on your merits, not the darkness of your skin.

But, wait! It gets better. The businesses that survive will then hire employees, who will be able to afford to borrow to buy homes, who will then be able to use equity to finance their own businesses and educate their children. Black wealth increases and success spirals out of control.

We might see the emergence of two or three Einsteins, 10 Tiger Woods, four or five presidents and a few dozen CEOs of billion-dollar companies. Possibilities arise exponentially when a community has a base of wealth.

That can't happen with a 10 to 1 ratio of economic inequality. Without the housing, food and educational certainty enjoyed by most white people, the black community will remain under siege.

As stated, creating a new financial system will be one of the most difficult tasks of all. As with most of the challenges facing the 21st century black community, the first obstacle is primacy – white people blocked us both from working in the industry and receiving its benefits. We have created some black banks, but they are small and lack the scope to be considered financial industry game-changers.

Here is what our New Banks would do:

- Loan money for mortgages, businesses, education
- Hold our money in a variety of accounts
- Insure our lives and our belongings
- Serve as an exchange for investment
- Facilitate bill-paying
- Eliminate the thievery of disparate lending practices

It certainly could take the approach of the banks who shunned us; the founders could accept our deposits, build huge vaults, buildings and security forces. The only difference is the New Banks would actually work for us instead of against us.

But, in the 21st century, there are ways to do all that in a more streamlined fashion. Use mobile banking to cut down on overheard, crowdsource the loan and insurance processes and encourage intra-group lending.

Mobile banking works. It's been proven in Kenya, Ghana, and Japan that consumers don't need to carry sheaths of dollars to make their necessary purchases. We are acclimated to plastic and fewer and fewer of us need to venture into the marble-tiled lobbies of banks.

Crowdsourcing is simply using large groups of people to achieve common goals by having each person contribute just a small piece of the overall costs. In a relationship-based industry such as finance, the tools to vet loan prospects already exist through crowdsourcing.

For example, we could use our own social media, an 'Usbook,' to check on business statuses, owner character and prospects. Each bit could be done by an expert and the loan risk minimized. Minimization of risk is where white finance has destroyed a great deal of black wealth. Any honest financier will tell you risk can't be eliminated. But, with black consumers, the cost of that risk was astronomical.

There are actual cases of broken down houses being purchased by white speculators for $5,000, then charging black people $15,000 for the property – with a $5,000 down-payment. The white speculator eliminated his risk as soon as he cashed the down-payment check. In fact, it works out better for him if the buyer is late on the remaining amount, so he can foreclose and make even more money on the house.

Right now, in every major city in the U.S., there are black consumers who are paying interest on items for which the principal was long ago paid – $10,000 for $900 refrigerators that broke down years ago.

The New Banks could lead us even faster out of the financial woods if they are creative enough to try new things – for example, intra-group lending.

Intra-group lending is what east Indians, Hmong, Nigerians, Italians and other immigrant populations do to help their peers and families. It's an exercise in trust that allows the group to make lump sum payments to one of its members in need. That payment is paid back with a minimum of interest and then another group member will take a turn.

Trust is the big factor. With the New Banks focused on relational banking, they'd be able to point out those who may be trusted for the group lending. They would also be able to hold the money for a small fee and disburse it, via mobile banking.

The first challenge in creating the New Banks is determining the structure. It needs to be flexible, yet sturdy enough to handle the challenges of 45 million people making a dozen or more transactions daily. It's possible, but highly unlikely, that the process could be helped along by a sympathetic state legislature. Legislatures are able to signal to the federal government that they wish to establish financial cooperatives, which operate like banks, without the FDIC insurance. It happened with the legalized pot industry in Colorado.

Black financial experts need to be involved at every step and questions of security, cash storage and federal regulations must be answered definitively.

The second challenge is to bring in partners from around the globe that can shore up the New Banks.

New Banks founders should reach out to black South Africans, Kenyans, Ghanaians, as well as east Indians, to form international partnerships. Existing, white-controlled banks do this everyday. The financial industry is international and London, Hong Kong and Tokyo are among the many ports of call for our money. Critics will certainly take exception to a black-focused enterprise taking on global partners, but so what?

The only reason black people are subjected to different rules for the same games is to place us at a disadvantage. If solid financial systems are best established with global foundations, then we should establish such a foundation.

New Banks, of course, aren't just banks. They are financial exchanges, the backbone of a community. Under different names the New Banks provide cash, insurance, loans, investment, funds safekeeping and more.

If existing black financial institutions were able to plug into a global exchange dedicated to treating its customers fairly, they would be able to grow to Citibank and GEICO size. Even better, with international leverage, our nation within a nation would finally be able to improve economic relationships with African countries.

Native-born African Americans have only anecdotal relations with Africa. Some of our wealthiest – Randall Robinson, Oprah Winfrey – might invest in the continent. But, for most of us, we don't do as our Mexican friends do – send money out of the country to support another country.

Still, trusting the backbone of our new economy to South Africa, or Kenya, or Ghana, or Nigeria is a monumental step. It fulfills the promise of all those bits of red, yellow and green leather jewelry we wore with outlines of the African continent on them.

It feeds Africa's finances in a healthy way and builds our own economy up so that we alone control it.

Don't dismiss the element of control. It's the unspoken civil right we have long been denied. We've been allowed the shallow victories of 'potential for inclusion,' tactics such as Affirmative Action, the Voting Rights Act, Equal Opportunity. But, we have been blocked from control. Black farmers controlled their own destiny – they grew and raised the food all humans require. They were aggressively eradicated by a government and cabal of American racists.

Oscar Michaux in his genius knew that moving pictures would prove a formidable tastemaker in America. Still, he remained frozen out until his death and a nascent black movie industry was aborted.

Here's a true story from the 1970s: a respected former athlete, a black man, was named as a vice president of a bank in an Eastern state. His hire was based on the glowing recommendation of his former college coach and his own good character. He was the first black person hired into such a high position and his job was to manage small business loans. Among the many loans he approved was one to a black business – the first the bank had ever written. The small company failed and couldn't repay the loan.

The bank fired him for the sin of having one company, in his portfolio of dozens, go into default.

His story illustrates the 'perfection' double standard under which we labor. Black people and companies are not allowed failures. That is insanity. White people learn and grow from their failures. George W. Bush, Abraham Lincoln and a million more notables failed multiple times. But, they possessed the resources of family and finance to try again – and again. Drunk with billions of dollars of venture capital, white tech entrepreneurs espouse a strategy of 'Fail Fast, Fail Often.'

It is critical to our success and the success of our future generations that we let go of that impossibly high standard. The 'one failure rule' is as destructive as the 'one-drop rule.' If we can't absorb failure, we can't afford creativity. It informs much of the pathology of black people who have given up on the system. The majority of hard-working, honest and intelligent black people would say, if stopped on the street, that we only have one chance at financial success.

Most of the time, we don't even have the one chance. We had no voice in home loans, so we were legally barred. We had no voice in business loans and we virtually never received them. We have no voice in venture capital, so the latest iteration of robber barons will again be a cast of white men.

The 'One Failure Rule' has created a future for us that make the Sons of the South gleeful. Our businesses tend to be puny, we remain dependent on a white economic system that cheats us and we have given up on trial and error, because we can't afford it.

If we stay with the NASDAQ, the NYSE and the other pillars of Wall Street, we must expect the same existence for our children. They will fear failure as much as we do.

That's not the existence we want for our children. Barack Obama has shown them they can aspire to the highest heights, but without a safety net, our children's aspirations are lowered automatically. Denied the chances to fail and grow that white children take for granted, means President Obama could become the Tiger Woods of U.S. presidents. Our children won't be able to succeed him once he's done.

Hear that? That's music to ears of Mitch McConnell and the Sons of the South.

White Republicans know the tropes of black society – it's their pact with the Sons of the South. They study us so they may hurt us. They've worked hard to ensure their twisted view of President Obama takes hold. They've tried to brand him a failure, even if it means turning their backs on issues they hold dear.

Why? They are familiar with the 'One Failure Rule.' It plays well for the Sons of the South. They love to see a black man persecuted. But, the underlying hope they hold is that it discourages future Obamas from even trying.

Modern media has fallen in line with the false equivalencies and outright lies fashioned by the GOP. Republicans say the President failed to reach out to them and the media parrots them, wringing hands all the while. But, how do you reach out to someone who wants nothing to do with you?

A generation of young black men and women grew up witnessing the relentless attacks on a dark-skinned man simply doing his job. It's a sobering lesson for any black child who aspires to those heights: the depth of racial hatred shown by some white people.

But, we can use our parenting skills to fix those impressions. We've addressed a billion such slights over the generations. If we set up the structure to better our economic lives, the racists will simply be engaged in busy work. If they can't block us from buying decent homes, earning strong wages, properly educating ourselves, all they have is name-calling. 'Nigger' loses its sting when you out-earn the ragamuffin shouting it at you.

So, it is crucial to set up the New Banks and secure our financial future. Until then, we will focus on absurdities. Silly comparisons will abound, such as: "the average dollar circulates 20 times in the Jewish community, but only once in the black community."

In the paraphrased words of our yellow brother Homer Simpson, "Well, d'uh."

Such comparisons will always be silly – apples versus oranges – when we possess only a patchwork of tiny, service oriented businesses to claim as our own. Most Americans spend money on groceries, cars and upkeep, homes, clothing, entertainment and telecommunications.

We don't have a strong presence in those industries, so how is our dollar supposed to circulate? There are only so many bean pies we can buy.

Our $1.3 trillion buying power will be an afterthought to the exiting financial structure unless we create the New Banks.

That leads to the third challenge…

Expect Resistance

Who will try and stop us? Search for 'Wall Street' on your computer and every organization that comes up will be a culprit. Do the same thing for 'federal government employees' and you'll be on the right track.

This enterprise requires smart, talented, sophisticated and globally-focused leadership. Money is the center of this project and it is the same stuff that powers our government and our industries.

Multi-billion dollar companies exist because they killed or bought up their competition. The New Banks are competition. White companies will aim millions, if not billions, of sharp dollars at the heart of this creation. They will do their best to kill it.

A trillion dollars in buying power is a lot of money. That's the size of black buying power at this moment. Financial companies will fight dirty to keep it, despite the fact that simply treating you as equal to white consumers would have accomplished just that.

Capitalism isn't necessarily the enemy, but those in power are wielding it as a weapon against us. American capitalism in its 239th year rewards size and money. It has grown a few behemoths in each industry that are 'too big to fail.' It's why we have six food producers, four media companies and three car manufacturers for a nation of more than 330 million people.

Two-hundred-fifty years of capitalism is why the old tools of the Civil Rights Movement don't work today. Try as you might, you can't boycott the Koch Brothers or Cargill or ADM or Fox. They own so much that all roads lead to them. You can avoid certain brands of toilet paper and Fox News, but there are other brands owned by Koch, other programming offered by Fox. Avoiding them is a full-time job when many of us are looking for full-time jobs.

These are the types of companies that will be up in arms at the "uppity" nature of our collective decision not to follow their path.

Government will act first to squash the New Banks. They will enforce obscure regulations within inches of their lives. They will find fault with the backgrounds of the creators and enact new laws to make it difficult to build black-friendly financial institutions. They will deny permits, zoning, contracts – any "legal" thing they can.

What they don't deny, they will delay. Delaying gives government's Wall Street masters time to come up with counter-responses.

Financial companies will try to buy out the principals of the various New Banks – by either hiring them away or paying them for espionage.   They will try to undercut pricing. They will try to duplicate the process by creating black-friendly financial institutions that could have easily been created in the 1960s.

And, of course, they will sue and blackball. The lawsuits will be based on whatever legions of lawyers can come up with, while the blackballs will be phone calls to their like-minded friends with the simple message, 'Don't work with these people.'

It will be the 1950s all over again; financially powerful white men working to shut down the 'black menace.'

Their Resistance, Our Response

Put our money where our mouths are. Between government intervention and a hailstorm of Wall Street dirty tricks, even Mother Theresa would cast a sideways glance at Jesus if He was the Founder of the New Banks.

Our haters will tell lies to prevent the New Banks and unless we fully participate with our dollars this enterprise will be steamrolled.

We need a critical mass of true believers investing their dollars right away. A million black people demanding the service of New Banks won't stop the resistance, but it will lead us to a place where some small protection is afforded – public relations.

It isn't possible to shame American politicians or bankers, but harsh public relations situations do give them pause.

Consider Min. Louis Farrakhan's Million Man March back in the early 1990s. White people in power did not want that to happen. White media coverage was negative or dismissive, but the Nation of Islam didn't rely on those platforms to get the message across.

When it became obvious that hundreds of thousands of black men would, indeed, deny their programming and travel to Washington, D.C., there was nothing left but to sit back and fret. They fired their biggest salvo after the March's completion. The U.S. Park Service informed the white media that the march had failed because fewer than a million men participated.

The media ran with that story. It collectively trumpeted that 'only' a few hundred thousand people actually attended.

There is a lesson to be learned. The light of publicity can inhibit some reprisals. The Million Man March, in the eyes of the Sons of the South, should have never happened – but it did. The New Banks can definitely happen, but the most dangerous phase will be their set-up.

The Congressional Black Caucus is a natural shepherd for this delicate process. It will also be a test for that much-maligned collective. Do they have the independence necessary to do something no black organization has ever been able to do in America's history? Protect black people from powerful white interests?

Too many black people consider the CBC impotent. What have they done for us, lately? Well, lately is now.

Technically, the CBC has the power to point to black international partnerships and guide us through the minefields of legislative opposition. But, will they do that?

A thousand defeats have been snatched from victory's jaws for us. The CBC is filled with pragmatists who accept money from people they wouldn't invite into their homes. Many of them are funded by the same interests who will want the New Banks dead.

This is where the rubber hits the road. If enough members of the CBC profess their allegiance to their community, the process stands a chance.

CBC silence will be a high wall to climb. If no support exists on Capitol Hill, it will take longer and be a bloodier fight. It will still be winnable, but it will lean solely on the numbers of true believers and our foreign partners.

South African banking, just as an example, would be a strong partner and allow the New Banks a toehold in a foreign market where the U.S. reach is weaker. We'd pay a premium to be sheltered from white resistance, but in the long run, it's worth the cost.

Once the New Banks are set up, they much harder to tear down. U.S. government efforts to topple a foreign, black-friendly financial system would be an overreach. And, U.S. imperialism is getting tiresome even to our allies.

We hold all the cards when our New Banks are set up. Like Israel and Mexico, we'd be an economically sovereign nation that is able to use its money to benefit its people. Shedding the capriciousness of a financial system that hates us will do wonders for our collective self-esteem. More importantly, it will literally save the lives of many of our children.

Black America has been forced to create underground economies to feed, shelter and clothe our families. With the advent of the computer, American government, courts and law enforcement have attempted to squash any of our efforts to counteract racist economic exclusion. They made numbers running illegal for black people, but were oddly unable to prevent the Mafia from doing exactly the same thing. Then, they made numbers, now called the lottery, legal for states.

Drugs were introduced into our communities from white organizations – the Mafia, the CIA, Latin American cartels. Italians, spies and politicians are, again, untouchable. They become as rich as kings, but our young people go to jail.

Our history has been to be close to the large fortunes that we make possible – but we are shoved away and the door slammed when it's time to count the cash. When rap started to make real money, record executives swooped in and made billions. Tupac and Biggie were shot dead, leaving their families to fight over the scraps of their estates.

The Sons of the South and their believers keep a sharp eye on our money. If a segment starts making too much, they move in to prevent it.

It's time to understand and shout out loud that these people are traitors to America. They are fighting American citizens – us – in attempts to deprive us of our Constitutional rights. It's time to fight that battle head on. They consider it a gift of their freedom, part of their God-given rights to stymie our progress.

They've lost and lost badly before. Their losses have exposed their true nature: they skulk and move in the dark to achieve their aims. They work with hate, code words and dog whistle racism. But, we are a people comfortable in the light. Our goal of achieving our own happiness is the true American dream. We have fought and won our freedom against unthinkable odds. We beat them twice before in Civil War I and Civil War III. We can kick their asses in Civil War IV and be done with their evil once and for all.

Then, we must be ever vigilant and take a page from post-Holocaust Jews. We will have to declare, 'Never again.'

Instead of being analyzed and studied by our enemies, it will be *our* turn to keep the Sons of the South under a watchful eye.

Chapter 5
'Just-Us': Creating Our Own Legal and Law Enforcement Systems

Son, do you know what I'm stoppin' you for?/'Cause I'm young and I'm black and my hat's real low?/Do I look like a mind reader sir?/I don't know/Am I under arrest/ or should I guess some mo'? – **'99 Problems,' Jay-Z**

Tackling media and finance will be business-focused tasks. Very large companies will want to squash the competition for our money, which they see as theirs but temporarily in our pockets. They will bring government subordinates into the fray, but they will be the principal opponents.

That will be less true for our other big challenge – creating our own legal system, a 'Just-Us' system, in the words of the late Richard Pryor. Our major opponent in this endeavor will be the U.S. government.

Creating a Just-Us system will fly directly in the face of the American legal system. A system that has tried us, convicted us, imprisoned us and murdered us for centuries. We are their "best customers."

The current American legal system is the hammer of the Sons of the South. Media mollifies us, the financial sector robs us, but the legal system murders us, literally – with its death sentences and killer cops – and figuratively through broken families, crushing debts and societal lockouts. It's little wonder that many of us consider incarceration to be the new slavery. Our police departments were founded on the concept of rounding up runaway slaves.

The first collective use of policing in America was for slave patrols, roaming bands of white men who sought to violently capture runaway slaves. They were called slave patrols and their methods of reconnaissance, tracking, identification, and interrogation became American law enforcement. Slave patrols begat police officers riding in "patrol cars." Michael Brown's murderer, Darren Wilson, wasn't an anomaly; he is a direct descendant of the slave patrols.

It is a system that has killed innocents, deprived families of loved ones and officially sanctioned violence against us.

From Eleanor Bumpurs to the Simi Valley jury verdict travesty to Amadou Diallo to Trayvon Martin to Oscar Grant to any number of 'disappeared' black men and women who were taken away because of the misnamed 'War on Drugs,' the legal system has never offered justice to black men and women. Racist judges regularly and actively void the Constitutional rights of black people. It's happening at this very moment.

At the very top of America's legal system is one of the black community's most staunch opponents. U.S. Supreme Court member Clarence Thomas would be a sad joke, if not for his position. He has done more than a thousand-year KKK terror campaign to roll back the rights of black people. His robes should be white with a pointed hood. He is symptomatic of a system that defends "corporate speech" and gay marriage at the same time it strips black voting rights.

Thomas is the cautionary tale. He sits on the court to signal there is no more help coming. We have to do this by ourselves, because black people like Thomas are so wounded they see no other path but capitulation to white supremacy.

Most of us have no dealings with the U.S. legal system, but that's not for lack of trying on the part of its officers. We are stopped and frisked, jailed for minor traffic incidents, truancy and child support in an ongoing campaign of community harassment.

Just-Us would be an oasis when compared to the 'accidental' shooting and choking deaths we suffer at the hands of zealous law enforcement.

We need Just-Us badly. Its absence is a reminder of another way the Civil Rights Movement didn't make our citizenship equal to white

Americans. White people don't fear the justice system as we do. They are given the benefit of the doubt and treated with some degree of fairness.

Our own fear is extremely rational. There really is a bias against you and those who look like you. Race may not be scientifically real, but racism is pretty solid.

What is irrational is why a people would submit to the whims of such a court. It's as if Jews submitted to the laws of Nazi courts. Here's a fact: when the Civil Rights Movement won Civil War III, the Sons of the South recognized the power of the courts in those few moments when the system sided with the oppressed. They then filled the courts with conservatives who disliked black people.

They did it quietly. Every lower court position that opened generated a fight in support of their 'law and order' candidates. Little did we know that phrase introduced the newest code for racist behavior.

Before too long, presidents Reagan, Bush and Clinton had turned the U.S. into the world's largest jailer. Black men and women were enslaved, filled America's jails, creating jobs in small white towns and inflating the telephone bills of families hoping to stay in touch with their incarcerated loved ones.

Little has changed today. We are locked away for any and all infractions. Despite having the same drug use rates as white Americans, we are 10 times more likely to be jailed for that crime.

America has told us for 250 years 'There will be no justice for you!' Maybe not. But, there is room for Just-Us.

Let's not ignore a reality – some black people will not conform to societal norms even it the society is black. It's human nature and to be expected. Then, there are the traitors, the Clarence Thomases, Ward Connerlys, Michelle Malkins, Stacey Dashes who possess a white supremacy mindset.

These people are psychological realities. Most will die embracing their misguided beliefs. Of far more concern are the millions of black people who have given up hope for something better. They can be reached, but not easily.

Whole families, whole generations of families have come to the – reasonable – conclusion that they may as well do the worst they can do, because this thing isn't going to get better.

They take to crime because there are no jobs to be had. They kill other black people because those are the people within pistol range. They are indifferent to their children because they can't protect them from the hard lessons soon to come. They lie, cheat, steal and use drugs.

They can't wait to die.

It's a hedonistic lifestyle that's fueled by self-hate and hatred for both white and black societies. The white hatred is based on the crimes perpetrated against them and the black hatred is based on the impotence of the community in protecting them.

These are the people who need Just-Us most. They need proof before they die that there is fairness in the world.

In a society where death sentences claim innocent lives and police officers approach jaywalkers with drawn pistols, that will be a hard lesson to teach. Many won't buy it. But, it has to be done, if not for this generation, then for the next.

Our goal should be a total removal of black criminal and civil cases from the white legal system. Our self-policing should be absolute.
- If there are property disputes – Just-Us.
- If there are custody disputes – Just-Us.
- If there are estate disputes – Just Us.
- If there are physical assaults – Just-Us.

We have the power to create a legal process that is simpler and a million times less punitive. Instead of calling 911, a peacekeeping arm of the system would respond to certain emergencies on a rapid-response basis ahead of the police force.

It would be founded on true community policing – not the spy network that is the true intent of current community policing.

Such a system would offer victims protection, but also allow the accused to feel that true innocence has a chance of being uncovered.

In civil matters, dividing estates and the properties of dissolved relationships would be settled with equal weight considered for both parties.

Thousands of reports alleging police brutality are filed annually in America, fewer than a handful result in even a slap on the wrists for the officer-perpetrators. Creating a Just-Us system removes us from beneath the hammer and establishes a truly fair system for black people.

We create Just-Us with massive amounts of cooperation and planning.

A new 'Continental Congress' is required to set up such a far-reaching system. We'd use best practices to establish it. Hard questions, such as, 'Will the enforcement arm need weapons?' 'When, how and why do we jail our own?' will be tackled.

Importantly, what is the mechanism that we use to exact retribution from out-of-control police officers? The answer to that is crucial; it signals our commitment. Whether it is setting up a snare for bad cops – for example having a young black man walk where they don't expect him to be and then flooding the area with black faces when he is unlawfully detained. Or, do we keep track of each and every interaction with black people by each and every cop and have the bad ones fired? Perhaps it is some combination of both.

These thorny questions can be resolved through our collective genius in state-by-state federations. These federations will have multiple leaders, clear succession plans and goals. Each success will be shared with groups from other states, until the process is ready for a national vote.

Then the continental congress takes over and ratifies the system.

The founders of Just-Us will engage in two fights at once. They will struggle to reconcile the complexities of the new system and they will have to combat the existing legal system.

Oddly enough, the first supporters of the process likely will be conservatives who favor law and order and believe black people will treat members of their own community as badly as the existing system treats them.

It will give them an opportunity to say something positive about a black community they don't care for – after years of paying lip service to an Hispanic community they don't care for but need for political survival.

Their supportive statements will deflect a bit of the obvious racism some of them exhibited during the Obama Years.

That verbal support will end when the numbers are crunched. Allowing black people to take a hand in their own justice will certainly shutter for-profit prisons and gut the slave wages paid by any number of large companies relying on prison labor. Factor in small town prison closings in places like Terre Haute (where it has long been rumored that white supremacist guards torment the black inmates) and working class white people are sure to lose jobs and livelihoods.

Fewer cops will be needed on police departments, which will have police unions up in arms.

As ever, white racists value our bodies – as prisoners, perpetrators and free labor – but not our minds. We will give notice that those days are done by saying, 'We control our destiny.' Then all hell will break loose.

Suddenly, 'separate but equal,' will be re-examined and found wanting. Apologies will abound, promises will be made with no intentions of follow-through. They will tell horror stories about rampant black crime leading to society's breakdown – all on the backs of Just-Us.

Their real issue with us will be that we are seeking post-Civil Rights Movement control of our fate. Their system is predicated on handling us one-by-one. It can swallow individuals whole, steal their homes, families and lives as easily as the Pennsylvania Juvenile Court judges, Mark Ciavarella and Michael Conahan transformed into degenerates who sentenced children to detention in exchange for money.

Individually, we are vulnerable. Forty-five million strong, we are a nation. As heady as the centuries of white supremacy have been for some white people, even the most power-drunk among them understands no nation can jail 45 million people. One either declares war or comes to the negotiation table.

A hot Civil War V would be a disaster for the Sons of the South. There would be no more darkness to cloud their true motives – subjugating black people. The PR calculus would be impossible to solve.

It's reasonable to assume a majority of white Americans would balk at a war against black people trying to improve their lot.

Entering a war in which you are never certain of loyalties is a recipe for a devastating loss: see Vietnam, Afghanistan or any Islamic conflict. Generals might have black girlfriends; Aryan-looking captains might have beloved black grandfathers. And, the foot soldiers and techs? There are endless potential sympathies – crushing on Michael Jordan, life-altering moments courtesy of Oprah.

Plus, a shooting war on American soil will bring out the nuttiest of the white supremacists who will eventually start shooting at their government allies unless they declare race-based slavery as their final solution.

The world will watch this freak show and nations like China (which has extensive investments in Africa), Russia (which really doesn't like us), South Africa, Saudi Arabia, Brazil, Mexico and Canada will make decisions that likely won't be in support of a racist, imperial regime showing its undisguised true colors.

It's very conceivable that the UK and Israel might offer aid, but neither are world conquerors.

Will it get that far? Unlikely. Still, trust that racists will engage in thought experiments that take the scenario that far. Their control over us defines who they are. Without us, they're not even white, anymore. They are a collection of former Germans, English, Irish, Italians, Poles and Swedes who will have to find another scapegoat.

They might decide to discriminate more against women, or maybe the Italians. But, we are their dream scapegoat. We are instantly visible and are too long removed from our ancestral homes to have sovereign protectors.

They have worked for centuries to get us to this supposedly vulnerable point, but they have underestimated our strength of character. We have a million Michael Jordans – alpha males who refuse to lose; we have a million Shirley Chisholms – alpha females who knock down any hardship you throw at them and overcome them on their own terms. We are 45 million strong and no matter how much we are ignored; no matter how much attention and money the 'largest minority group' – Hispanics – receives, we are not going away.

Some white people in America have tried to destroy us. The unintended consequence of their actions is a stronger, more adaptive black American.

That strength will be the fire that fuels the Just-Us movement. We are blessed by the fact that we don't need permission to create any of these systems. That is particularly true of the Just-Us system. The legal system can bitch and moan all it wants. So long as we are collectively involved and agree to the terms of Just-Us, it is constitutionally protected behavior.

It is no more illegal than the Mormon Church essentially running the state of Utah, despite there being a Constitutional restriction regarding separation of church and state. Still, the U.S. government looks the other way.

They won't look the other way for us. They never do. But, we don't need them to in this instance.

Expect Resistance

White Americans have been acculturated to a legal system that doesn't treat them well, if they're not wealthy, but still has pockets of fairness. That has never been entirely true for black Americans. What shocked white people most about the original O.J. Simpson verdict were the new rules it introduced. Black people with money were now above them in the legal system.

That didn't sit well. It was inevitable Simpson would eventually land in prison to put their minds at ease.

Many white Americans are very comfortable with the way our legal system discriminates against black people. There are a select few who advocate against the wholesale execution of innocents, but those cases are a few hundred out of a million or more.

Jail time for drug possession, drug use or hundreds of other non-violent crimes is fine with most of them. They don't see the fear the system causes or the families it tears apart.

It's unlikely that liberal white people will join in for this cause. Their call will be to fix the existing system with the Pollyanna statement that, 'It's not a perfect system, but it's ours.'

They are unaware how thoroughly conservatives rigged the legal system to target black people. It is broken beyond repair. From judges that are paid to send children to detention, to D.A.R.E. programs that cataloged tattoos, family relations and street nicknames in a system of surveillance, to a racist black member of the Supreme Court, the product is rotten.

We face the most fearsome of resistance when we embark on this path. Thousands of sons of Theophilus Eugene "Bull" Connor will appear to stop us. And, they have learned that disappearances, dogs, nightsticks and water hoses are bad PR.

They will tout the rectitude of the legal system, point to the Civil Rights Movement's court victories, knowing full well that those couldn't happen today. They will label the Just-Us movement as black separatism, with no mention of the separation a million incarcerated black men and women must feel from their families. The legal system will be held up as a shining example of all that is good and right in America and the Sons of the South will employ its dog whistle rhetoric. It is good and right, except for black people, and that is how they want it.

The back-channel resistance will be even stronger. The legal system will use its privileged societal position to coerce former prisoners, politicians, business leaders to fight dirty against the competition. Blackmail, threats, theft – all illegal – will be used in unironic defense of the legal system.

The nation's legislatures will also rise to the defense of their cousins in the judiciary. Laws will be made requiring adherence to the existing legal system and millions will be spent on campaigns to sway public opinion.

Their Resistance, Our Response

Martin Luther King. Mahatma Gandhi. Henry David Thoreau. Rosa Parks. They were all practitioners of civil disobedience and that is the best tactic when embarking on the deadly task of toppling kings.

We must understand that that is what happening. State and federal politicians, judges, prosecutors, law enforcement, big business administrators all see themselves as kings. They aren't truly answerable to the public, while we hoi polloi must accept whatever decrees they throw down from on high.

On our side is the fact that history is full of Mandelas, Cromwells and Washingtons. They have led a hundred Marie Antoinettes to their respective guillotines. We can win if we keep our eyes on the Just-Us prize.

Black-owned social media should be our best friend in this particular struggle. Every black person wronged by the justice system should air their grievance in public: black farmers who sued the USDA and lost, those who had their properties taken on a technicality, targets of discrimination who lost winnable cases, incarcerated innocents, should all make their cases public online.

A massive argument demonstrating the racism of the legal system doesn't have to sway white people; it needs to remind us the system is irreparably broken. We will see we have no choice.

Then, we can go topple kings.

What kings forget is that they don't exist without a kingdom. It is amazingly difficult to keep a kingdom together. And, when a particularly powerful duchess, say, one with 45 million followers, decides she wants to go a different route, all a king can do is try to save face.

The most important instruction the creators of Just-Us have to follow is, 'Stay the course. Work the plan. All will work out.'

We need to trust and believe in Just-Us. Most importantly, we have to allow its judgments to be recognized as valid.

Walls fall all the time, the fall of our broken legal system will make for one of the most satisfying piles of rubble, ever.

Chapter 6
Reconcile Our Men and Women

*Just when I think/Ive taken more than would a fool/I start fallin'/
back in love with you –*
'Fallin,''' Alicia Keys

There are more industries we will have to create, but they will hold for a bit. After setting up black-friendly media, financial and justice systems, it will be time to take a breather and consider how we interact with our new social mechanisms.

Older heads will eventually adjust, but black children will quickly immerse themselves in the new. That fact demands we set a social structure that speeds the process along. The New Media, if it's created properly, will bolster their self-esteem.

What will then be required is the face-to-face dissemination of knowledge that humans have relied on for millennia. Our mission will be to save our boys and love our girls so they may enjoy healthier relationships than we were able to manage.

Boys will grow into strong black men that make and stay in homes with strong black women and healthy black children. We do that by creating community-wide rites of passage – like Jewish Mitzvahs and Mexican Quinceneras.

As ever, we don't need to re-invent the wheel. Some great rites of passage already exist within our community. Organizations such as The Links or 100 Black Men have cotillions and transition events that would translate wonderfully well on a broader stage. One or several of those events could be used to shuttle our young boys and girls into adulthood.

It is not a trivial ceremony. Life left to its own devices is a poorly organized existence. Relying on biology and physical urges to signal the transition from childhood to adulthood is a messy proposition.

Commencing adulthood transition is much easier with clear baseline behaviors set and expectations attached. We have flown by the seats of our pants for generations because we could never count on what tomorrow would bring: we woke up slaves, then we woke up free; we woke up celebrated; then we woke up reviled.

Establishing a baseline means we see what the reality is – and adapt according to community needs. For instance, we might have 30 percent unemployment. That would be the reality, the baseline. We'd resolve that issue, because we are numerically aware of it. We might find that 30 percent of our adult men and women are married and collectively choose to consider that number too low and shoot for 70 percent marriage rates. Baselines are necessary to show progress or failure.

It's part of the reason so many white organizations don't want to collect racial data: data collection can provide solid evidence of racism. Police departments don't want to gather racial data on traffic stops. Colleges want to stop collecting data on the racial make-up of their student bodies. It allows them to plead ignorance of discrimination.

They call it being colorblind, when it's really stonewalling.

We'd establish as many relevant baselines as we could for our young people. We'd want to know about their education, job training, relationships with each other, goals, aspirations, financial levels.

And, we'd compare that snapshot in time to a later snapshot in time. No white people are required. We'd measure our progress against ourselves.

Simple measures such as establishing rites of passage and setting baselines inform us about ourselves. They transform our relationships with each other. We've always waited for white-generated numbers to be released, so we might better know our wretchedness. Those numbers told us we were unemployed, soon-to-die, virtually blocked from certain colleges and institutions.

Power flows from those who determine the numbers. We deserve that power. We don't need to ask for it. We can take it and use it.

Its best use is changing our relationships with each other. If we recognize and celebrate our successes, we create new realities. We will still have hardships, but those hardships will happen within an overall context of positivity.

We are a culture that prepares our sons and daughters for manhood and womanhood with no fanfare. That should change.

What else should change is our estrangement from each other. Black men and women have ridden rough seas for at least a century. The love is there, but it's tattered. One of our Community Holidays should be a Day of Reconciliation between men and women.

With 70 percent of our children born out of wedlock, there are any number of issues to reconcile:
- Are fathers paying adequate support for the children?
- Are fathers spending time with their children?
- Are mothers badmouthing the fathers?
- Are mothers preventing fathers from seeing their children?

Those are just the issues faced by men and women who have children together. Interracial romances, bad feelings over women out-earning men; there is a long list of items that should be aired out.

The second community-wide holiday we should create? A day of thanks for black women. There's an old saying that "mother" is a baby's first word for God. If we don't acknowledge the incredible pressures borne by black women, we weaken black men by sparing them the truths of what their distaff halves endured.

It would be a fairy tale to simply wait for newly-strong black men to return and fix centuries-old problems as if it were as easy as hammering shingles on a roof.

Women stood their ground and saved our community. They nurtured us with hope. They believed in black men when black men didn't believe in themselves. Without black women, we didn't – and don't – stand a chance to grow into something even greater.

Black men should make it their life's work to thank black women for their amazing perseverance. And, adding a darker-skinned Mother's Day won't do.

Our event should be reverent, worshipful and strive to atone for the soul-crushing behaviors aimed directly at black women.

Every human suffers heartache, but black women have been smashed over the head with it from within and without. These strong women endured the 'Baby Mama' era - legions of black men refusing, through their actions, to raise families with them. They watched their sons disrespect women as if their mother weren't female and standing there.

They were forced to work, take care of children, forego meals and accept being called everything but a child of God. Rap videos depicted them as shifty gold diggers for so long and so diligently, that the catchphrase, "We don't love them ho's," easily crossed over into the mouths of white men like radio host Don Imus. Imus couldn't believe calling a group of black female basketball players 'nappy headed hoes' was controversial.

After all, black men did it all the time.

To our shame, he was right. Many black men stopped marrying black women; grew enamored of the Bishop Don Magic Juan pimp lifestyle – taking much more than they ever gave. They surrendered fatherly duties to the state or whoever stepped up.

No. A simple 'sorry' won't cut it. The only resolution is to rebuild black society with women seated at the table they purchased with their blood and toil. Black male resentment is not allowed. You don't thank your savior by saying, 'I could have done it myself.'

That's not gratitude. That's testosterone talking. It gets in the way of building new media, financial and legal systems. It blocks the progress of an emerging, powerful generation of black children who will be at the wheel steering a 21st century America into the 22nd century.

Gratitude should come with a ring for those who resisted jumping the broom. Help her pay her bills and raise your children. Feminist Gloria Steinem gained fame for her quote, 'I refuse to marry while in captivity.' She may have been right, but captivity is a lonely space. And, Steinem did marry.

Love between black men and women will be deep and honest, going forward. There is no other way to proceed. Black women have seen and experienced too much to sit in the back of the wisdom bus. That means our five-percenters, American Muslims and OGs have to find a way to accept the reality that our new, cohesive families will be both patriarchal and matriarchal.

You might ask, 'What if my mother is my problem?' What if the things she did held me back from being a better person?

If that is truly the case, you may not want to celebrate her. But, human relations are tricky. Your mother may have been a hooker/drug addict that slept with men to feed you and took drugs to dull her own pain. She may have been young and ignorant and couldn't empathize with your needs. She may no longer have the same mindset she had when she was younger.

The decisions we make under duress are hard to explain to those we have wronged, especially our children who are unable to see them through adult eyes because they aren't adults.

It is always your choice to participate and, perhaps, in participating you and your mother might have a real conversation and resolve some issues.

So, yes, there are some bad mothers for whom this will not and must not apply. They were intentionally neglectful or abusive and refused to change as they aged. Maybe they gave in to the hopelessness of their lives, but that was the choice they made and the consequence was their children leaving them by the wayside. Still, they are the extremely small minority.

The vast majority of black women have been to war. They've raised enough men to know violence and ugliness firsthand. The black woman's voice has to be equal to the black man in setting our collective future.

That future has to be built to support a 21st century black child who possesses the best of every phase of the black community in America.

Our children must have the survival will of the earliest enslaved Africans; the adaptability of the Reconstruction era, allowing them to quickly engage new opportunities; the unity of the long-lived Jim Crow era, when we trusted and depended on each other; the bravery of the Civil Rights Movement warriors, who recognized and fought injustice despite being outgunned; the entitlement to freedom of the post-Civil Rights generation; the technological savvy and curiosity of our turn-of-the-century youth.

That is a potent combination.

When we achieve it, we will have scientists, physicians, researchers, scholars, engineers and mathematicians better represented in our community. We may drop significantly in our representation among professional basketball players – just as the Jews of the 1940s did – but it will be fine. We will own teams to make up for it.

Our children will be more technologically-minded because that is the direction the world is headed. An information-overloaded world will increasingly rely on technology to solve its complex problems.

Racism blocked the collective genius of our ancestors, leaving their potential untapped. With that cap removed, our next LeBron James will be a rocket scientist calculating Mars colonization missions.

All this happens by embracing the unfairness of our past and melding it with the future we desire. We need to exploit the physical aggressiveness of our young men and women and plug them into both mental and physical pursuits, equally.

Instead of dodging 350-pound defensive linemen, our talented girls and boys will be reflexively protecting themselves from those who mean them harm, as well as expanding humanity's knowledge.

There are those in the community who might see rites of passage, gender reconciliation and reparations to black women as window dressing, something that can wait until later. They are wrong, wrong, wrong. These actions are central to the community moving forward.

We have been so traumatized by American racial politics that we have a well-known phrase for the secrets we keep. We call it 'airing our dirty laundry.'

Director Spike Lee and several prominent black celebrities are famous for airing that dirty laundry. But, the wise person knows that laundry gets dirty and we are not doing ourselves any favors by keeping these open secrets.

White people already *know* some black people are prejudiced against darker-skinned black people. That's not news. Their system was instrumental in creating it. White people *know* some of our men and women are trifling. That's simply being human.

It is a by-product of the One-Failure Rule that so many of us can't accept hearing about our shortcomings in mixed company. If we wait for a black-only conference that is away from the prying eyes of curious white people, we will wait forever.

The present system didn't become so effectively destructive by accident. A certain segment of white people has always paid attention to us. Observations about aberrations like extramarital affairs and drug use became child support and drug laws that have imprisoned hundreds of thousands of us.

A certain kind of white person will always listen to what we're saying. At this moment, there are white people reading this book and taking a great many more notes than you are. Their aim is to disrupt positive change.

Our goal is not to hide away our conversations, in some outdated notion of privacy that hasn't existed since the invention of the transistor, but to wave our dirty laundry with pride and shout, 'I know you're watching! I don't care! You can't stop us!'

The best revenge for our ancestors is to have the Sons of the South realize that truth. They can't stop us. They will no longer contain us.

The strategy behind creating a new attitude among our children starts at home and extends into the classroom and workplace.

Twenty-first century black America will need a panel of Dr. Spocks to relay the wisdom of raising a new generation of black children. Dr. Benjamin Spock was an influential pediatrician who wrote books on child-rearing at the height of America's Baby Boom.

That tactic will work even better with a black-owned internet available to generate best practices through trial and error. Instead of being the final arbiter on what parents should do, our panel of Dr. Spocks will be challenged and, often, corrected.

Every black parent should have access to the information provided by this panel. And, the panel should use a Consumer Reports model – no advertising to tilt the findings.

Parents should also form alliances to discuss the real-world application of each suggestion. Neighbors should talk, as well as family members and other concerned adults. The talks should be both formal and informal – cups of coffee and 15-minute check-ins, as well as hour-long, weekly educational progress reports.

With the parental involvement of black America dialed up to 11, the black child will be in a spot she's never been in America – the center of positive attention.

Questions will beget questions and the answers will rain down. That attention will then extend to the classroom.

That is where the hard questions need to be answered: what are the best ways for our children to learn? Are teachers' unions helping or hurting my child? Should we create our own institutions, effectively re-segregate ourselves?

The problem with traditional education is it wastes the potential of too many young people. It can create the odd Ann Fudge, Michelle Obama, Lonnie Johnson or Neil DeGrasse Tyson, but without a higher success rate it establishes a second-tier elitism that fosters intra-community resentment.

It's the reason we have jealous children accusing certain schoolmates of 'acting white.'

This is the first beat walked by the racial policeman in our heads – attack aspiration and tear down intelligence. It happens in the white community, all the time. But, there is an urgency to this particular dysfunction in the black community.

It is telling that it has been effectively eliminated in the Jewish community. Jewish mothers want to know, early on, if you are going to be a doctor, lawyer or engineer. They want to see nothing but vowels on your report card and could care less about your cool factor at school. They know where you are going to spend most of your life – in adulthood. And, in adulthood, societal contributors – doctors, lawyers, engineers – get the best perks.

We need to continue the celebration of our bodies and populate sports leagues with talented athletes, but, by a ratio of 20 to 1, we should be also celebrating our minds.

It is psychologically obvious why so many of us denigrate academic success. We might believe that it's an attitude that separates from our oppressors; in the words of the street, 'Fuck them honkies!' In reality, it's a vestigial behavior from slavery and Jim Crow that clears the competitive landscape for future white doctors, lawyers and engineers. We supplied the brawn in the fields; they used their brains and privilege to reap the spoils of our labor.

They have long had their own league, a non-athletic league that is 10,000 times more lucrative than any NBA or NFL. In that league, they continue to keep out brilliant black minds with a well-oiled series of obstacles. Guidance counselors discourage us; schools put us on non-college educational tracks and for those who make it past the obstacles, the workplaces brutalize us. Tech industry founders have created gargantuan companies with about as many black employees or partners as they have on the AMC drama "Mad Men."

And, they are disingenuous enough to say there aren't enough black computer science graduates to add to their virtually all white and Asian ranks. But, numbers make liars of them. A white computer science graduate is more than twice as likely as a black computer science graduate to be hired by the Facebooks and Googles and Twitters of the world. A study has shown that racial hiring bias exists even in fields that are screaming for technologically trained employees.

Affirmative Action is despised by a certain segment of whites because they prefer the much older, Negative Action system set up to thwart us. *Of course*, we weren't supposed to be there. The doors were clearly marked: 'Do Not Enter.' It has nothing to do with merit and everything to do with melanin.

Since we can't force white people into a post-racial mindset, we have to create our own supra-racial future, meaning 'beyond the limits of' race. We will be supra-racial through our own efforts. Owning one's own home is supraracial. Earning a good wage and providing for our families is supraracial.

Best of all, the path that leads to it is all within our reach.

Expect Resistance

Embracing reconciliation and celebrating the strength of black women will at first be seen as a no-brainer, even by most white people. The opportunities for companies to market their wares will attract the merchant-minded.

They will rub their hands and conduct market research to find out the best cards to sell. It is in our favor that they miss the point of it all.

Reconciliation and celebration will foster the healing of our souls. It's not a marketing bonanza. Selling 'reconciliation travel getaways' would be as ludicrous as selling "South African Truth and Reconciliation Commission Silly String." It will certainly happen, but it's still ridiculous.

The early grumblers, white people who don't want to see black people take charge of their own fate, will make the first negative comments. They'll use the hoary argument they use against Black History Month: "It's not necessary. We're all Americans."

But, as the positives evolve and escalate, the usual White Citizens' Brigade will start to worry. Law enforcement, courts, politicians will see their business drop off as black solidarity emerges. Then the resistance will begin.

Stories with no point of origin will suggest sinister motives for reconciliation and celebration. These apocryphal tales will declare that someone is being paid big money behind the scenes, making suckers out of black people. In some of the stories the perpetrators will be black, in others they will white.

These lies will reside on the white internet under reasonable-looking banner ads and spread like wildfire on Facebook.

The reality is they began here, in this book, in this chapter, with no other motive than black people have grown tired of lives full of post-traumatic stress syndrome. We need to take control of every aspect of our lives in order to thrive for the rest of the century and into subsequent ones.

Luckily, hating on a healing black community – one with less crime, better jobs, gang disputes resolved, higher marriage rates, healthier and happier children – is a PR trick shot. The haters must balance obviously positive events with a destructive message that reeks of racial animus. How does one translate 'black educational achievement is bad for America' into a rallying cry for the 21st century?

Their Resistance, Our Response

Positivity is the natural armor for this set of strategies. The twice-defeated Sons of the South don't have the power to enact the blatantly racist laws of yesteryear. So, they repurposed. Their 'no literate slaves' laws are now under-funded public schools.

The biggest obstacle for them is they no longer have the power to come into black homes and simply tear down whatever they choose. So, this set of ascendancy strategies is home-based. They may be implemented wholly by the black community. We don't need Hallmark or Wal-Mart to make it happen.

That's why whisper campaigns, devious internet and broadcast stories will be the enemy's front lines.

Trouble is possible if we try to farm out the aims of these strategies outside of our community. We have everything we need to build what we need. And, we'll write our own mortgages on our own futures.

Still, it's necessary for a community group to remain vigilant and keep an eye out for the aggressive haters. Touchy-feely happiness in our community is bad for their business. Setting the foundation for a generation of high-functioning black geniuses means they will be forced to actually share the wealth with dark-skinned people.

That will mean billions, or even trillions, more dollars in our community. It will mean the original Affirmative Action, the Good Ol' Boys Network, will die and money will be earned on the basis of merit.

Don't underestimate the depths to which racists will go in order to horde money. Yes, there are some white people who would rather lose money than treat black people fairly. But, remember, slavery was about money. The perverse power over fellow human beings was simply an addictive part of that devil's bargain.

Since the early days of slavery, American racism has always been an unholy mix of emotional immaturity, power and greed. Ten generations after Civil War I, no one has ever offered a rational explanation for the Southern Pride – read, anger – Sons of the South feel about fellow human beings freed from a living hell. Some have even stated publicly that black citizens should thank white people for the privilege of their ancestors being kidnapped, stolen away from their homes and forced into free labor to enrich white Americans.

To understand 21st century racism, one has to be a student of emotional retardation and avarice. Luckily, many in the black community are PhDs when it comes to the motivations of haters.

A broken legal system, ironically, provides the best protection black men and women could possibly desire. The most direct way to combat strategies of reconciliation and celebration is to outlaw them. But, there will be no such luck for the Sons of the South.

The American legal system has evolved to jail black people, not intervene in community-wide celebrations. If it could act on celebrations, Kwanzaa would be a goner. But, that Afrocentric holiday has existed for years on the doorstep of Christmas.

This set of strategies will not be struck down by any legal means.

Still, it bears repeating: some of the community's organizers should remain vigilant to any and all opposition, developing a threat matrix and the responses needed to combat those threats.

Chapter 7
Understanding the Opposition We Face

No hope/I'm shackled/plus gang-tackled/By the other hand swingin'
the rope/Wearin' red, white and blue/Jack and his crew –
'Can't Truss It,' Public Enemy

If we conduct our business reasonably well, the early 21st century
will be boiling with black industry. Amazing missteps and fantastic
successes will occur daily. The fiery anger of creation will form
enemies, friends and frenemies galore. But, if the pursuits stay pure,
everything will be worth the cost.

What's important is to be impatient with the process – within reason.
Impatience is important because the creators of the new 21st century
likely won't see its full evolution. Still, it needs to be an impatience
that demands quality.

Toward that end, it's important to define white America in new
terms. Don't let your eyes glaze over; this isn't a busy-work
exercise. Re-defining white America also reveals the extra-
community obstacles that challenge our rebuilding.

The process of defining shows us some of what lies ahead, suggests
potential pitfalls and when we make the separate calls to action for
the various projects, it allows those who sign on to do so with open
eyes.

Racial clarity has never been America's strength. It's important that
we fully and truly learn the lessons that have always been in front of
us. The election of a black president offers a master class in the
examination of white American attitudes.

President Obama's America provided daily lessons over the course
of a decade on the power of racism over white people. It's been said
by millions of commentators, but it bears repeating: conservative
white people lost their minds.

Racial hatred made them do stupid things. White politicians supported bills until the President publicly agreed with them; they then turned against their own bills.

Republicans sent out pictures of the First Family as gorillas, monkeys or eating fried chicken and watermelon on the front lawn of the White House. When they were busted, each and every one of them was shocked that people considered them racist.

An entire billionaire-funded movement, the Tea Party, arose simply to block anything the President did. Whether he wanted to appoint federal judges, support a healthcare bill that became law or even take a vacation, Tea Partiers were angry.

That anger had very little to do with the President's policies. It existed because President Obama was a black man. Worse, in their eyes, he was a black man born of a white mother, which meant a black man slept with a white woman. It was the lynching trifecta.

Racism so rampant and blatant couldn't be swept under the rug, so white conservatives kept busy pulling out old Jim Crow tricks for the 21st century.

The oldest trick in the book is to blame black people for racism. Black people are now called racist for any and all "transgressions," including:
- Voting for President Obama,
- Calling out disrespectful behavior towards black people,
- Fighting discrimination and
- Protesting the murders and other injustices of the American justice system.

Here is the 21st century state of race relations: a large percentage of white people do not want you to have anything. Period. They begrudge you your home, your car, your job, your relationship, your citizenship.

And understand this; they cannot be accommodated. If you accept a poorer home, a bad car, a subsistence job, they will want you to have less.

It is the Obama Effect. They wanted to impeach him for doing his job.

That is the distilled essence of racism. And, it won the day for them in the 2014 mid-term elections. By doing nothing, and despite the economy getting better, gas prices getting lower and the federal debt shrinking, they won by labeling their failures as those of the President. There is no logic to refute racism; there are only actions to take. Talking to most racists gives them a chance to stall while planning dirtier deeds.

That is another reason we should be impatient with our implementation – the odd behavior directed toward the President caused a shift in attitude for many white people. They openly longed for the days of legalized racism. They expressed, for instance, their hatred for "political correctness." But, like "states' rights," that's a well-worn racist dodge that actually translates to "I hate black people."

A small, but determined minority of white people are trying to figure out how to roll back civil rights for one very special group – black people. They should be rebuked with every ounce of communal energy. They are laughable human beings, but their cause is not a joke. It is seriously possible for America to find its way back to a pre-Civil Rights era. It happened in Civil War II (Reconstruction) and Germany surprised the majority of its citizens when it legalized hatred of Jews.

The racism our children deal with is different than that of our grandparents. It resides, undiluted, in a much smaller group of white people, but the gene remains in most white people.

Racism's vilest aspects are still murder and plunder, but those extremes are rare enough now to dominate news cycles. Racism is slickly systemic with a variety of effects born of "no causes." Eduardo Bonilla-Silva terms it, "racism without racists."

They believe higher black unemployment exists because black people are not as skilled as white people; movies have few black actors because they are not as talented as white actors; black people don't make as much money as white people because they choose the wrong careers. None of it is the fault of the system.

To prove that America is not racist, media shows us daily how much white people love Hispanics and gays. It's kind of like a woman showing how much she likes you by kissing on your brother.

The implicit message is, 'We are tolerant; there's just something wrong with you.'

If the black community continues to listen to those types of messages, insanity will claim millions of us. It's called cognitive dissonance by psychologists. It thrives on mixed messages that eventually absolve the message-sender of blame and forces the message-receiver to question his sanity.

There is nothing wrong with the black community that the black community can't fix. Like all "minority" communities, it has a world-shaking capacity for power. Minorities possess the power of cohesion. Being lumped together forces discussion, cooperation and understanding.

Cohesion allows smaller groups to dominate larger groups. Witness Jews in the media or Saudis in the oil trade. Think about this: globally, white people are a minority with an outsized impact.

Recognizing this, certain types of white people live in abject fear of black collective will. Murderer Charles Manson went on his killing spree because he wanted to foment a racial war. He felt that if the black power movement wasn't squashed in its early stages, black people would run the country.

He was right and he wasn't alone in his conclusions. The FBI and a host of other government agencies came to the same conclusion. They enacted the Cointelpro plan to spy on the Civil Rights and Black Power movements and slaughtered fierce opponents, such as Huey Newton.

What an empowered, 21st century black community requires is a more strategic skepticism of white people. Many white people gravitate to racism because it elevates their status, something every human feels he or she deserves. It takes an unusually developed mind to recognize the subjugation of other human beings and decide it is morally wrong. The prospect of an unearned, elevated social status leaves a small band of white sociopaths unreachable. And, in an age of willful ignorance typified by The Simpsons and Family Guy television programs, highly developed minds are rarities.

Types of White People
There are four primary groups of white people in America, Smiling Liars, Dittoheads, Sons of the South and Beneficiaries. Our goal should be to more effectively recognize and deal with every type.

Smiling Liars
Smiling Liars are those who know they are telling untruths about black people, but do so anyway. These are the talkers, not actors. They are the employers who walk you through interviews they never mean to consummate with a job offer. They are the ones who accuse the President of crimes like being an illegal alien. Their favorite phrase when busted is, "Some of my best friends are black." SLs are a step removed from KKK membership because they won't attend rallies, burn crosses or physically assault black people. They don't like black people, but are able to camouflage that hate in front of other white people. Conscious black people recognize them on sight. They do most of their damage in all-white groups whose members think the SLs are racially disinterested. Given power, they are Antonin Scalia, of the Supreme Court, who described voting rights protection as an "entitlement," or Ronald Reagan, who turned the War on Drugs into a prison recruitment plan for black drug users.

Hollywood is a Smiling Liars playground. The industry has the power to change racial attitudes substantially just by hiring more black actors and having black films mirror the diversity of experience showcased by white films. Instead, they choose to perpetrate negative stereotypes.

Dittoheads

Dittoheads don't think deeply and often parrot what Smiling Liars say. They are a larger group and more interested in their own issues than race and politics. While not actively anti-black, they are often steered into positions that hurt black people. They are against Affirmative Action, equal opportunity, President Obama, political correctness and welfare – but 'not because of racism,' they say. They just see these things as "bad" for America.

Dittoheads can be politically left or right. Again, Hollywood is home to a lot of Dittoheads, despite conservatives labeling the industry as leftist. Studios rarely feature black artists and then only in carefully defined roles that don't upset the status quo.

Black workers in the industry all have dozens of stories about racially-specific rejections: 'Black movies don't do well overseas.' 'My white client won't tour with a black man.'

Disney, alone, has spent hundreds of millions of dollars in an attempt to turn back time. Its TV programs and movies for tween audiences rarely feature black people – and the ones that do put them solidly in the background, mostly as comedic relief. This is the programming that will help shape minds for an audience that represents the first American generation since the 1800s to be comprised of a white minority. This is the main lesson Disney wants to teach the next generation of Dittoheads: black people are best kept in the background.

It is difficult to pin malicious intent onto Dittoheads, because they are racial followers. So long as the mail is delivered, the grocery stores are affordable and there's something good to watch, they are comfortable in the neighborhood of white supremacy. They won't initiate, they barely participate and their only moral certainty is that there is no systemic attack on black Americans.

Sons of the South

These men and women possess a soul-deep hatred of black people, despite, in many cases, never interacting with any black people. They are the ones who will act on their antipathy. One of the greatest positives of the Obama administration is that we have been able to positively identify them.

- Congressman Addison Graves "Joe" Wilson (R-SC)?

He broke more than two centuries of protocol and shouted 'Liar!' at President Obama during his state of the union address. He is a Son of the South.

- Sen. Rand Paul (R-Ky)?

He said he is against the Civil Rights Act. He is a Son of the South.

- Former Deputy Police Chief David Borst and Officer George Hunnewell?

They are Missouri police officers who were outed as Ku Klux Klan members during the Michael Brown demonstrations. They are Sons of the South.

Every Tea Party member and Republican politician who shared racially offensive posts and pictures on the internet and all those who bad-mouthed our Commander-in-Chief have shown their true colors as Sons of the South. They set the stage for militia groups intent on killing the President and for "teachers" like Gil Voigt of Fairfield, Ohio who told one of his young black students, 'After Obama, we don't need another black president.'

SOTS can camouflage themselves as Dittoheads and Smiling Liars, but they can't help exposing themselves when the rubber hits the road. For them, few other issues in America are more pressing than the oppression of its black citizens. In positions of power, they create voter ID laws to combat voter fraud in a country where barely half of us vote; they insist on mandatory sentencing for drugs that black people use. They research welfare, child support, drivers licenses, any and every government program they can, to see how best to use the power of governance to oppress black people. They want to pass laws that prohibit people on food stamps from buying steaks.

Those who are not in power, hiding behind screen names, will go to KKK and neo-Nazi websites to have their hate validated. They make racist comments on YouTube and Twitter on any story with a black or political angle. They belong to the hundreds of hate groups that sprang into existence after the President's election.

These are the enemies of our state. They are the domestic terrorists that Dittoheads and Smiling Liars describe as 'over-exuberant.' The sickness in them is sociopathic in nature; they are the sons and daughters of murderers who regret only that their racist murders are no longer officially sanctioned.

There is a stark difference between black people and Jewish people when it comes to our enemies. Jewish people still pursue the killers of their people. Nazis in their 90s are found and brought to justice as part of the community's 'Never Again' strategy. Many of our killers walk free and unrepentant. The Jewish community's attitude must be carried over if the black community ever wants closure.

Beneficiaries

This is the largest group of white people and the demographic that most angers Smiling Liars and Sons of the South. Beneficiaries don't actively despise black or brown people; they are indifferent to most things outside of their comfort zone. And, unlike the Dittoheads, they don't succumb to the blatant propaganda of the SLs and SOTS.

The SLs and SOTS can't understand such an attitude since it means that they and their children will lose an historic advantage by being forced to compete fairly with black people.

White privilege isn't a central concern of the Beneficiaries; it's simply their environment – they are fish; it is their water. They share a common trait with black people in that they are simply trying to make it through their lives without demonizing other groups.

They are working to pay mortgages, raise children and afford creature comforts. Unlike most black citizens, they are able to live obliviously. When they're not hired for a job, they don't second-guess the racial motives of the interviewer; when they are rejected for a home loan, it's not because of collusion between the government and the real estate industry. It's because they weren't selected based on a set of fair and transparent rules and competition didn't favor them in that moment.

They are free to dust themselves off and try again, likely to some success. Their strongest connection to racism is that they are beneficiaries of the practice. It's pushed them to the front of the line so many times in their lives they see it as a normal wind at their backs. They internalized it, assuming it is part of their mental talents.

Beneficiaries do what black people would do, if given the opportunity. They accept the advantage. SOTS, Smiling Liars and Dittoheads attack Affirmative Action efforts because they try to weakly replicate for black people what American society automatically confers upon white people.

The toothless Affirmative Action law's requirements are fulfilled if employers simply interview black candidates. They can then hire a staff comprised completely of white men and be considered compliant with Affirmative Action goals. Still, the fact that the tech industry – the first iconic industry of the 21st century – is virtually all white proves those 20th century racial lessons were well-learned. Again, black people have been shut out on the ground floor of a major capital-generating industry.

Beneficiaries operate in a world where white has been the default setting for so long, it is considered a force of nature. Many black people have succumbed to that thinking, as well.

But, being a habit doesn't make it a truth.

Neutralizing the New Racism

The necessary strategy for community ascendance is to identify and actively fight the programs of the Sons of the South; identify and discredit the Smiling Liars and Dittoheads and to observe and refute the entitlement of Beneficiaries in a non-combative manner.

Ironically, the most difficult struggle will be with the Beneficiaries, who will see a black community building solidarity as a threat. They will see it as a threat because they see nothing wrong with the government, media, employment, housing, healthcare and legal systems already in place.

'Why fight something that's benign?' they will ask.

Answers to that question will be whispered into their ears by SOTS and Dittoheads: 'Black people do it because they hate you and don't trust you.'

Some Beneficiaries will become Dittoheads or, worse, SOTS. But, those few must be considered casualties of Civil War IV.

One of the most powerful weapons against virulent hatred will be The Database. It will negate the Sons of the South's biggest advantage – invisibility. There is a saying from a movie that goes 'the Devil's greatest trick is convincing us he doesn't exist.' With The Database in action, the invisibility of the Sons is no more.

We will see them for who and what they are – and that greatly diminishes their power over us. Moreover, it gives us power over them. We are able to track their movements, uncover their plans and alert others to their intentions. It is the nightmare scenario for the Sons of the South. When they cry, "We're not racists!" black America will reply, "Yes, you are. And, here's the evidence."

That is a power we have had only in fits and starts in America. Paired with the construction of a black-friendly media/economic/legal infrastructure, SOTS shenanigans would transform into the sound of gnats buzzing. They'd be minor annoyances shooed away with a wave of the hand.

Twentieth century racial attitudes need to be destroyed. We can no longer afford the lives and money lost in support of white people feeling superior. Look at the reality. Sons of the South have a great many white people asking, 'How long do black people get "special treatment?" at the exact same time white people in power are trying harder to keep black people oppressed.

Any logical person would respond, "What kind of 'special treatment' would leave a group on the worse end of every societal indicator?" And, the logical answer would be *negative* special treatment.

There have never been clean intentions toward black equality. Welfare drove our men out of their homes to find jobs when there were no jobs to be had. Affirmative Action helped far more white women than black people. The California university system's "colorblind admissions" rules decimated black student admissions, but when it became clear that Asians were bumping out an inordinate number of white students because they possessed better grades and test scores, the powers-that-be decided to "fix" the new problem.

The only consistency has been that white people maintain an advantage. That's not news.

What is news for a 21st century black community is we collectively have the tools to neutralize racism and create a system that can immunize us from its future effects. The Database. New Media. Just-Us. All of them work to approximate the Jewish-Mexican model of self-sufficiency, which in turn is an approximation of a sovereign state.

There are many resources that favor an empowered black community. Most of them were apparent to Marcus Garvey and Huey Newton decades ago and Cudjoe, leader of the Jamaican Maroons, centuries ago. Those resources are resilience, intelligence, individual talents and moral strength. What Garvey, Newton and Cudjoe lacked was advanced communication technology.

The Civil Rights Movement was mapped out on the backs of envelopes and at the tail ends of Sunday services. Activists connected by wearing down the soles of their shoes and gathered at the behest of wristwatches and calendars.

They were blocked from knowing the internal workings of banking, government, and media. They were mere consumers who grew into righteous citizens strong enough to withstand bullets; strong enough to tear down the industries that kept them at the back of the line.

Because of those warriors, the system changed.

They had no idea of how to take advantage of that new reality. But, we do.

Because overt racism is considered bad, much of the new racism is disguised. That leads to the grand irony: the Sons of the South are forced to hide their true motives just as generations ago our enslaved forefathers were forced to hide their true motives of seeking freedom. It is a small but poignant gift in honor of our ancestor's struggles.

The process of hiding motives dilutes power. Hidden motives are why much of 21st century racism involves arguments about the existence of racism.

Frustrating as that is for the good guys, it signals extreme opportunity for community progress. Money has won out in America and the one-percenters dictate their demands to our political, legal and, of course, economic systems.

There are enough Beneficiaries and Dittoheads that we have the opportunity to create a new wealthy caste of American. These Beneficiaries and Dittoheads are white Americans who see green in certain instances instead of skin color. They respect their black bosses and the landlords and lenders who hold the keys to their economic well-being. If you have money, you have their attention.

Sons of the South and Smiling Liars are inclined to fight against their own economic self-interest to ensure that black people are left with nothing, economically. But, they are in the minority.

We are sitting on roughly two trillion dollars worth of wealth, about 1/40th of overall US household wealth; based on our population numbers it should be closer to 12 trillion dollars. Still, if we collectively insulate our money and grow it exponentially, we will be able to control our destiny in ways never before possible. America will then truly be our land of opportunity. No longer will the latest wave of immigrants be considered fully assimilated when they learn to hate black people. Black people will be the welcome committee, the employers and neighbors.

Sons of the South and Smiling Liars – even the governors and CEOs – will be forced to the bargaining table with us or be swept into the dustbin of history. They will be compatriots of the Jew-bashing haters who whine, yet still pay to use their products.

Our greatest enemy will have fallen for a third and final time.

It is impossible to keep a giant demographic down forever without the help of its members. Public Enemy had it right: 'It Takes a Nation of Millions to Hold Us Back.' Unless we keep doing the holding for them, it can't be done.

What we have to avoid are the 'colorblind' traps set by Sons of the South. They want to dazzle us with the colorblind society concept described by Dr. King, but they wish to pervert it and turn it into a Brazil-type colorblindness.

Brazil has the largest population of Africans outside of the Continent, but those African-descended Brazilians are not featured in the media, have no voice in politics and are dirt poor. Worse, they haven't experienced a Civil Rights Movement of their own. Many black Brazilians accept the lie of equal opportunity despite there being no facts to support it.

White Brazilians sound like American racists when they insist there is no racism in Brazil. Those white Brazilians are not colorblind – they are willfully blind.

Black Brazilians are a few generations behind black Americans in terms of equality and would be well-served by witnessing the next phase of black American growth.

America's rush to pure capitalism has trampled human rights but, as mentioned, affords black America a chance to upgrade. Malcolm X famously opined, "What does a white man call a black man with a PhD?

"Nigger."

In our upgraded, post-Obama America, the question becomes, "What does a white man call his black boss?"

"Ma'am."

American democracy and capitalism have not outgrown racism, but it can be managed with enough capital. White Americans have less and less of a connection to whiteness as the struggle to survive gets more expensive on US shores.

If black industry provides better entertainment for less – they will buy it. If black industry offers better food for less – they will buy it. If black industry offers a new product they desire – they will buy it.

Where racism is the most potent is in preventing black industries from forming; dashing the dreams of talented people such as Oscar Michaux. In white-favored settings, there is little to no chance of their creation. Banks won't lend to black businesses; venture capitalists won't invest in ideas presented by black people and white customers are discouraged, in myriad ways, from patronizing black businesses.

But, black-generated industries have a crèche they can use to grow and learn. It is the trillion-dollar black community. Still, that can't happen without a plan and a core of participants. SOTS have thrived by preventing black collectivism since 1619, but at this late date, the only insurmountable obstacles are those we create for ourselves.

Will the black community decide to overcome the evils perpetrated by the Sons of the South? Certainly. Even if not one idea in this book is implemented, the power of the black community will win out.

But, it might take 200 years instead of 25.

Sons of the South have always touted the virtues of patience – for us. In the meantime, they rapidly monopolized all the tools and pieces of industry and society. They rushed into the Industrial Revolution, forming robber baronies, building cities, racing into space.

All the while, they warned us to slow our roll when it came to equal rights. 'People just aren't ready for that,' they'd say with faux concern. Apologists for the Old South have grown fond of the lie that the South would have eventually freed its slaves without Lincoln's intervention – if only we had been more patient.

'Don't work together,' they say.

'Take it slow,' they caution.

We did so, without ever considering the real reason for their warnings.

Not working together is simply participation in the Roman empire-building 'Divide and Conquer' stratagem.

'Taking it slow' gives them more time to grab control of society and lock us out. We followed, to the letter, the worse advice in the world.

We only progressed when we grew "sick and tired of being sick and tired" and acted with impatience and collectivism.

That impatience and collectivism is necessary today – this moment. We need to decide who's against us and who's with us and inject black America with its own nation-building drive. The process doesn't need all 45 million of us, but it does need a core of believers and doers.

After its success is achieved, then the decision to permanently reject or include black Americans who refused to participate should be soberly considered.

Most importantly, we must discuss, ad nauseum, the reason for embracing a self-directed capitalism and creating a massively parallel democracy. Our revolutionary brothers and sisters from the 1960s and 1970s would be appalled at a plan to work within a corrupted economic system as opposed to destroying it. Capitalism and democracy are tools of the oppressors. After all, the 'revolution will not be televised.'

Much love and respect to Gil-Scott Heron, but it must be televised… and Tweeted and Facebooked and LinkedIn. Except those social media services must be black-owned and operated and we have to be the primary audience. Our challenge is magnified if we try to create 1950s Red China in 21st century America. Changing the narrative of our ascendance from "collective will" to 'communism' plays to the strength of the Sons of the South – they would then resort to blatant lying to foment fear.

Even progressive Beneficiaries will view communism as a threat to the American way of life. They will never equate massed industries such as media, farming, petrochemicals, etc., as threats. But, a group of lower- to middle-class citizens banding together to right wrongs is easily labeled a mob. If the mob is black, the negatives are an easier sell to many white Americans.

We can be sophisticated about capitalism and democracy and not sell out the souls of black folks, if we so choose. That balance requires intelligent discussion and fine-tuning on the fly. The best way to do that is with modern communication methods that we control.

Chapter 8
No Fear: Failures Make Us Stronger

Fear is weakness/learn from what experience teaches –
'Self-Conscience,' Prodigy, ft. Nas

How many times has a plan, however small, worked perfectly for you? Closing times change, road construction eliminates parking, people become ill and there goes that perfectly planned vacation.

Ghosts in the machine affect every human endeavor. You could make the world's greatest plan to walk out of your house at precisely 8:01 AM only to find your clock stopped – or you could just drop dead. They say God laughs when we make plans.

Perfection is a rarity for anything that involves large-scale planning. Remember, rockets exploded and people died in our space program despite NASA employing regiments of actual rocket scientists.

We have to allow ourselves what white people take for granted: course corrections. Most plans aren't perfect, but well-thought-out plans get you close enough to success that you can cross the finish line. Astronauts died, but NASA made it to the moon. Our forebears lost powerful icons in MLK and Bro. El-Hajj Malik El-Shabazz, but we got the Voting Rights Act passed and diluted racism.

Most of us over 40 and black in America know from experience that our first chance has usually been our last chance. That terrifies some of us; it paralyzes many of us. Perfection is a pale beast with an appetite for our failure.

We can barely stand failing in solitude, much less having to look others in the eye and say, 'I was wrong. Let's try this a little differently.'

That needs to stop immediately. Get counseling or go cold turkey, but fix that attitude. If we see each failure of this complex process as ultimate failure, we will be wasting our time.

Failures provide information on effort, strategy and the competition. That is crucial data that can lead to lasting success. Individual examples are numberless. Abraham Lincoln failed before his ultimate success in being elected president. Dr. King failed in his early efforts to drum up support. Oprah Winfrey was a middling talk show host before getting her plan right.

And, on and on.

Collective failure also has a rich history. US history is a fascinating read because it a series of cliffhangers generated by the ignorance, incompetence or bad luck of our nation's founders. George Washington, for example, was a notoriously poor General. He lost most of the campaigns in which he engaged. Despite a legion of failures, they hung on long enough for the American Experiment to take hold. In other words, they reached their goal with imperfect plans.

That happens every day. But, our community has had that message scrambled because – again – black collectivism is a frightening prospect to the Sons of the South.

All our plan really has to do is reach clearly considered goals in double time. Just-Us doesn't have to eliminate incarceration on Tuesday, so long as it exists, points us in the right direction and allows us to make fixes. The New Media doesn't have to generate blockbusters right away, so long as it remains solvent and grows with messages of black empowerment. The Database doesn't have to rival Google in its technological sophistication, but it should work and do what it was built to do.

It's not just the plan. It is effort and follow-through that create a pro-black, post-Obama America. The goal of our grand plan is to segue from mandated consumers to self-actualized producers. Again, Gil Scott-Heron said it best: "All consumers know that when the producer names the tune, the consumer has got to dance. That's the way it is."

We've done enough dancing. It's about time we called the tune.

Do not take the mentally lazy route and characterize these admonishments as an ode to failure or a call for a lessening of standards. This is purely a reality check and a loving refutation of what our great-grandparents taught their children and grandchildren.

Our elders taught us that black boys and girls have to be twice as good as white people to achieve the same results. While that's a wonderful recipe for the Muhammad Alis and Susan Rices of the world, it's only viable for individuals that have the talent, drive, support and luck to be twice as good.

What we should have replied – in a respectful tone – is: "No. That's not fair. I don't want to be the CEO of General Mills. I want to work hard, make a decent wage, be happy and raise my kids. Why on Earth do I have to try twice as hard to do that? Did I do something wrong?"

Our grandparents' advice was based on love and a healthy mistrust of white people in America. The crazily unfair 'twice as good' standard left millions of wonderful human beings on the roadside. They might have possessed the talent, but their skin wasn't thick enough. Working 100 hours for something and then not receiving it, while a white person earns it with a mere 50 hours invested, is a huge fall. Magnify that hurt and anger when the time investment is 1,000 or 10,000 or 20,000 hours.

In the backs of their minds, all of those young men and women who gave in to the illicit drug trade calculated the 'twice as good' equation in their minds and correctly solved it – it is a formula for paying twice as much for the same things as white people.

No wonder they wanted the easy money of the drug and sex trades. Like any conscious people, they were tired of being ripped off. They decided to become outlaws. That outcome only surprises fools.

We can't afford to allow our best and brightest to give in to despair. The best fixes for an ascendant, 21st century black America is to let go of perfection standards and create a community-wide conversation about how to reach ultimate goals. The plan can change, evolve, stall, but, so long as it progresses, we are doing it right.

Another crucial factor is to encourage participation from as many of our 45 million as possible. Guaranteed, there will be amazingly cogent suggestions from youngsters or old heads without high school diplomas.

It would be a mistake to expect change to come from some talented-tenth without consulting those most affected by the changes.

In addition to the anti-racist dynamic of The Database, we must create a repository for both the stories of injustice and, more importantly, our methods to overcome them. Black writers in Hollywood must use their unique experiences to name names of the media executives who are raging Sons of the South and share every n-word, every sneer, every dashed creative dream so we know who to avoid when doing media business.

Homebuyers who are denied or charged exorbitant rates must share their horror stories of being steered to certain neighborhoods or being rejected while white people with lower credit ratings are approved so we ensure we never spend a penny with those perpetrators.

Students who hear racially discouraging words need to speak up and let us know the names of those teachers, schools and principals so we can act decisively to banish those dream-killers.

Black people are a forgiving people. That is both a blessing and curse. It is a blessing because it wicks off the bitterness of centuries of unfair treatment and allows us our good cheer and loving natures, but it curses us with a turn-the-other-cheek mentality as we deal with an evil group that has no problem perpetually slapping our faces.

It might be the heavy indoctrination of religion, it might have been centuries of no available recourse, it might be the vestiges of our parents' worry for our survival, but we often forgive as if we don't have a choice.

That is absurd. We can choose not to forgive. And, there are things we should choose not to forgive. If you continue to lie to our faces about our history, we should not forgive you. If you actively try to undermine the success of our community, we should not forgive you.

If you attack us ... We. Should. Not. Forgive. You.

White America has been spoiled by the habits of a religious-based Civil Rights Movement. The greatest white fear is that an eventual black reprisal will be commensurate with what they feel they'd do if the situations were reversed. What was one of the first things the anti-Obama crowd said after his election? "He'll take away our guns."

That sentiment is understandable, given their history of near-genocidal massacres of Indian men, women and children. Racists fear an empowered black community will re-create their history – the heads of men, women and children on spikes; arbitrary death sentences for minor offenses, removal of all rights of citizenship and a generalized reign of terror with the intent of subjugation.

Parts of our community do offer some support for their fears. Black-on-black crime will not always be black-on-black. De-humanizing thousands of black boys by eliminating father figures, disrupting their brain chemicals and providing murder instruction via videogames will quickly enough spread the mayhem beyond the inner-cities. The 'knock-out game' will evolve into the 'bust a cap game' and, like any game, the most points will be given for the unusual, the rarely-seen avatar, i.e. white people.

It's highly unlikely the conservative-run NRA will be as supportive when Newtown Massacres are perpetrated by black boys killing dozens of white victims – every week. But, the deeds will be done. And, the NRA, the FBI, the CIA, all of American government, will be as powerless against these 'suicide shooters' as they have been against the suicide bombers they've spent trillions of dollars and two wars trying to eradicate.

True hopelessness is a fuse and the explosions are ugly and radioactive. All races in America have been indoctrinated into the 'blaze of glory' trope: Butch and Sundance, Thelma and Louise, Bonnie & Clyde, George Custer and many, many more have all been held up as heroes.

Add hopelessness to that noble death trope, mix in centuries of racism and voila! America has created a counterpart to the white, right-wing terrorists lauded by the Sons of the South. We have then successfully brought Afghanistan home to Mississippi.

That is a wasted opportunity. Civil War IV doesn't have to be a hot war – though gun manufacturers would love the revenue. We may diplomatically avoid direct confrontation by uplifting our black community. It's part of our forgiving nature that we look out for those of us who are struggling. Like Harriet Tubman or the U.S. Marine Corps, we don't like to leave people behind, even if they're not our relatives.

We don't consider success to be a handful of billionaires while most of us live hand-to-mouth. America's politicians and business leaders failed us terribly in the Great Recession; they decimated our black middle class and flung millions into poverty. They then engaged the President in a series of mindless sorties around abortion, Bhengazi, gay rights and healthcare.

If we don't take action on behalf of ourselves, it will be 2214 before we feel truly equal in America.

Perfection becomes our enemy in planning our ultimate freedom if it delays us from making bold advancements. In a war, confusion and delay are powerful weapons. Our enemies are fighting a war against us that we haven't acknowledged, but we live on the battlefield, nonetheless. They count on stalling, obfuscation, lies and backstabbing to continue their string of victories.

Plans are fragile, abstract things that grow more fragile when the numbers of people involved rise. Stalling and lying are obvious ploys to destabilize black American collective effort. Our enemies know their payoff – subverting real black power – is too great to ignore. They will attempt to delay our progress with well-placed words and rumors, they will try to foster in-fighting so they may wreck the whole process.

We are remarkably vulnerable to that strategy because of America's history of white racial transgressions. They have spent centuries experimenting with the best ways to knock us down and keep us down and they've passed along the instructions from generation to generation. Even when we win, they change the rules of the game and cast our victory in doubt, as they did with Civil War III.

We must always compensate for our vulnerabilities – smaller numbers, less political power, less money – as we work our program of ascendance in the face of strong resistance from the Sons of the South.

The insidious, dishonest nature of the Sons of the South is on vivid display in their dealings with President Obama.

President Obama captured and killed Osama Bin Laden when his predecessor could not. But, our enemies credited only his weapon: Seal Team Six. President Obama captured the man responsible for the Bhengazi embassy killings, but our enemies said he took too long. President Obama, after six years of Republican obstruction, aggressively used his Constitutional powers to address untouched issues such as immigration, minimum wage hikes, gay and lesbian rights, black empowerment and presidential appointments.

The Republican Speaker of the House tried to sue him for it, despite the fact that previous Republican presidents had done the same things with their presidential powers – without threats of lawsuits. They labeled President Obama as weak for reaching out to them in compromise; they called him a tyrant for not compromising. They tried to drum up public support for his impeachment – in his first 100 days in office. They attacked his daughters for 'embarrassing the nation.'

The right wing went so far to block the President's agenda that it became as farcical as a Mississippi voting rights test. But, instead of asking potential black voters to precisely guess the number of bubbles in a bar of soap, a single Republican senator would show up in Senate chambers, bang a gavel in an empty room to call the senate in session, then 30 seconds later, bang the gavel to close the session and leave. The process would be repeated the next day with another Republican senator, called into Washington for the day by the party leadership.

The reason for this particular idiocy? A president may make recess appointments and put people into government positions without Senate approval if the senate is in recess. Republicans hated the President so much that they decided to never be out of session. Even if no business was ever conducted, even if only one out of 100 senators was present and even if the "session" was 30 seconds long.

Worse, the Republican-majority Supreme Court ruled that these 30-second sessions constituted a valid senate session.

That is the creativity racists possess when it comes to black people – and black presidents are no exception. It is a counterproductive use of labor, one that divides and weakens us as a nation. But, look at the results. President Obama's poll numbers plummeted and white voters rewarded the Republicans for not doing any work for six years by voting more of them into office in 2014.

They vilified the man actually working on behalf of 99 percent of middle class Americans. And, those who were blocking progress? They rewarded them with safer Congressional Districts and billions of dollars from the richest Sons of the South.

Do not misinterpret this message. Political messages don't come much clearer. White conservative politicians are saying, "We will not work with a black man. Ever."

That level of animus should demonstrate how badly we need to take control of our destiny. These are not the poorly dressed militia crazies denouncing some fictional 'sons of Ham.' These are the people in power, running our nation and passing laws that affect us.

They are Exhibit A through Z of our need to opt out of a broken system that will only tolerate us so long as we are subservient. Sound familiar?

There are doctors, lawyers, engineers and redneck rocket scientists in that group of haters. Their shameless sabotage and propagandizing are 1) planned, 2) racially motivated and 3) focused on an ultimate victory.

Those optimistic black people who believe the end of the President's term will get us "back to normal" are deluding themselves. It's not enough to have a white person back in charge. They need to see us punished. They will salt the Earth to prevent any possibility of another black president. They must prestidigitate and blame the President for their obstruction. Then, they have to pull a 'Tiger Woods' on the President and burn any and all bridges leading to another black president for at least a generation.

They will go after us with a vengeance as their reality 'snaps back.' With, at best, a Beneficiary in the White House, the old rules will allow for a new misery that will recall post-Civil War II days.

The Sons of the South will consider the Obama years as an extended recruiting drive. Their mantra of, "If you can't win fairly, change the rules," will kick into overdrive. Nonsensical laws, lifetime voting bans which, coincidentally, affect black people more than white, debtor prisons, illegalizing Reparations, legal racial discrimination in hiring and housing, will be on the table.

And, just like today, they will swear on a stack of bibles their actions are not racist. That's what they're supposed to say as combatants. They know they declared war and all their protestations of not being racist are bits of cognitive dissonance meant to defuse Beneficiaries and confuse the black community.

No.

In this climate, our enemies will resist anything that supports our community. Their relationship with the most powerful man in the world proves their intransigence. They will never work with black people.

Except when they need to suck up to power.

Mississippi Senator Thad Cochran (R-Miss.) has vilified black people in his decades-long congressional career. He branded black people as welfare queens and non-productive members of society. But, when an even more racist candidate appeared to his right and the Tea Party seemed poised to snatch the seat in a run-off election in June of 2014, who did he turn to? Black people.

He won because thousands of the black people he had disparaged and ignored possessed the power to vote him back in office. Thad Cochran was forced to swallow a bitter pill and acknowledge – in the deepest of the Deep South – he needed black people to help him.

That is the primary weakness of whiteness – there is no real solidarity in it, unless they are oppressing black people. Sons of the South know it. Whiteness cracks easily.

You could hear the howls of the Sons of the South all the way to Vermont. The irony, as ever, was lost on them, but the sons and daughters of parents who stole the vote from black Mississippians had their victory stolen away by the sons and daughters of those they had disenfranchised.

'You cheated,' they screamed. 'You got niggers to help you!' Cochran's opponent actually said "liberal Democrats," but the euphemism fooled no one.

That is our fate when we have our own systems in place. White people will break camp with the most virulent of their racists because a more powerful force beckons. We will be that force. But, only if we focus on goals and achievements, not pretty processes. We can then force any and all to come to us because we own the playing field. Jewish people have done it for years in America. As the media grew, so did their power. They may have been hated, but they were in the thick of the process of running the nation. They became kingmakers, despite being a minority.

There is no reason black people can't achieve a similar result. We are a larger population than the Jewish community, with more total money and thousands upon thousands of potential leaders who are able to guide us through treacherous waters.

In his book, "Capital in the 21st Century," author Thomas Piketty notes global economic numbers suggest emerging countries are catching up with developed countries. That creates an illusion of largesse on the part of the developed nations, he wrote.

"There is ... no evidence that this catch-up process is primarily a result of investment by the rich countries in the poor. Indeed, the contrary is true: past experience shows that the promise of a good outcome is greater when poor countries are able to invest in themselves."

Enacting these systems is an investment in ourselves and in our nation.

Expect Resistance

Sons of the South will invoke a tired catch-all, "the war on terror" when they see we are serious about improving our lives and lots. Though the usual cast of characters will be involved in fighting for our failure, the crews paid to eradicate terror will do the heavy lifting.

They will be operating under their usual orders – what's good for black people is bad for America. Bush and Cheney's wet dream of unlimited spying on and intimidation of average American citizens the Patriot Act – will come into play.

'Terror' will be the umbrella used to spy on and intimidate this process once they figure out the systems are all interconnected with a people's mandate to lift up the black community.

They will focus on the word, "collective" and monitor our emails, texts and phone calls. They will monitor the comings and goings of specific individuals and they will attempt to de-legitimize our efforts.

Because they give it the highest of their high priorities – a terror tag – government and business will align to do their worst. They will attempt to slow down or block our internet traffic and make our financial management difficult. These tormentors will wear many uniforms: SEC, FBI, CIA, Homeland Security and a legion of private businesses.

Their Resistance, Our Response

There is a Turkish proverb which translates to: 'No matter how far down the wrong road you have traveled, turn back.'

Our wondrous ancestors could not foresee the depth of duplicity modern Sons of the South possess. But, we have experienced it. We took a doctoral level course in it via their treatment of the President.

We have to acknowledge that we traveled down the wrong path to equality and must adjust our course. We control pitifully few of the levers of industry and thus are reliant on generosity and fairplay. That is capitalism's biggest myth – that it is a fair system. It is a system designed to allow the biggest to swallow up the smallest, a daily exercise in power grabs.

Power grabs are difficult for us because we only have a half-handful of black billionaires, a smattering of athletic and entertainment millionaires and a small army of millionaires in business, science and other fields. In America, fighting is about money. We don't possess enough for a fair fight because a majority of us have either miniscule or negative net wealth.

Certainly, when we make it into the fray as individuals, we can hit homeruns with the best of them. Get us into Harvard and we'll give you a president. But, there have been 15,000 white people who have attended Harvard over the years for every black student.

Post-Obama, they have grown comfortable rejecting qualified black people who apply to the elite schools that will determine the course of America's next few centuries. Facebook, Google, Instagram, Apple are all as white as if it were 1949. Their diversity extends to Asians and white women.

The path is blocked, again. If enough of us recognize that fact, we can cause some real damage to a broken system.

Our response is simple: survive. We are geniuses of survival. And, as we survive these new trials, we must protect our nascent systems. Necessity, as ever, remains the mother of invention.

When faced with wiretaps and other quasi-legal methods to destroy our progress, we need to tap directly into the strength of our Civil Rights warriors who held the flag high unto death.

Our freedom is imperfect, but that is not a denigration of our forebears' magnificent efforts on our behalf. The Sons of the South perverted the transmission of our civil rights because our ancestors didn't know what they didn't know.

Born a generation or more away from African cultures that would have accepted them, they saw being forced to pay more for housing as freedom; they even saw poor education as a gift. They considered the right to vote unassailable – once it had been granted.

We know better.

Housing, education, politics all enrich others who control the systems. They wield the power with generations of experience.

Our resistance has to be an iron-clad belief that even at this late stage in American history we can create our own industries. If we hold onto that belief and survive their onslaught, those industries will become real and productive.

Chapter 9
Turning These Words into a New Nation

Ready or not/here we come/gettin' down/on the One/which we believe in –
'One Nation Under a Groove,' Funkadelic

If *some* who read this book are 50 or older, we don't have a problem. We need the experience of those born in the 1960s and before. Those people are still bonded to dead tree technology. But, if only people who read paperback books are engaged, we have a huge problem.

Let's get it straight. You are not holding a book, you're taking in information. And, the way Americans take in most of their information today is online.

That is not only fine, it's necessary. These strategies are frameworks that require the genius of black thought to fully build. Look at them as if they were car bodies on an assembly line. They need doors, paint, windows and engines. Our young people already understand how to turn ethereal ones and zeros into real world action. Social media sparks flash mobs, concerts, protests and much more. The community needs their talent to plug into this information and add to it. Computer programmers call these collaborative models "open source."

That's the concept. Make apps and websites of the strategies listed in this book. Make them robust, interactive and enticing. Make them ours. Write about these projects in magazines; talk about them on Hot 100; feature them on talk shows; make fun of them on our sitcoms. Put it in the real world and enjoy the panicked faces of the Sons of the South.

Put the information in front of as many black people as technologically possible and the genie will be out of the bottle. Our pioneers will see it as a challenge and our community has a history of rising to challenges.

Young or old, male or female, gay or straight, rich or poor – just so long as the audience is black, the message will be getting to the right audience.

Some will accept it, some will reject it. The habit of blackness in post-Civil War III America has always been accommodating of acceptance or rejection. Light-skinned black people were able to slip society's racial bonds and enjoy the artificial advantages bestowed on those with white skin. Dark-skinned black people didn't have that option, but were able to align – not, join – with white interests.

Clarence Thomas of the U.S. Supreme Court would never be able to pass for white, but he has aligned powerfully with white interests and rejected the black community.

Accepting blackness in America has always been tantamount to rooting for the underdog. Because of our strong emphasis on the individual, we underdogs have often won.

Consider the cauldrons of black society and its creation of black achievers. Young scientists-to-be attend inferior schools and struggle against lowered expectations, peers who don't value scientific achievement, the sting of being labeled "white acting" and few avenues to exhibit their talents.

Young athletes, on the other hand, are pitted against elite talent on the fields and playgrounds – the sons and daughters of star athletes – and struggle to rise above the competition. Many more competitors are broken than become stars.

Young entertainers face the same brutal competition that athletes face, with the added difficulty that, except for rap music, there are precious few outlets for their skills in the white-controlled media.

Stars emerge from each of these disciplines despite the challenges. All of these young, individual talents are made aware by their families that a white system will work overtime to prevent their successes. It is a collective awareness that creates what we'll call a 'Joe Louis Effect.' Our young strivers will fight even harder against white faces, because that is the face of the constant opponent. Just as Joe Louis defeated a white 'superman' in his fight with Max Schmeling, our young achievers know they have to get an entitled monkey off their backs to achieve their goals.

Competitive black society ensures that select individuals can beat *parts* of the system. Still, as a system of ascendance, 'individuality uber alles' is a poor tactic. It ensures survival, but does little over the course of generations to empower the community.

But, we are blinded by lottery odds because our underdog does win – time and time again. Some of us are thrilled by those wins and accept the black community. Others see the stacked deck, consider the odds, and side with the white society – which is to say, against the black community.

It's pointless to try to win over black people who don't support the black community. There were Jews who supported Hitler, Muslim women who supported Shari'a law. There will be black people against black causes. Historically, those people were labeled traitors, but unless Civil War IV becomes something needlessly horrific, they may simply be considered lost souls.

They don't need to be 'taught lessons." They need to be left on their islands, much like Thomas who has the support of a few black Republicans and a few Sons of the South who don't view him as their equal. In a pitiful display of Thomas' racially awkward belief system, he has publicly anointed himself a "Civil Rights hero."

We have no need for the worn-out, tired and cynical - the Clarence Thomases, Ron Christies, Ward Connerlys or Stacey Dashes of the world. We need the message to get through to the young and impassioned. These young people will show old heads how quickly communication moves and how sticky it can be in modern minds.

They understand the concept of 'opt-out.' They won't waste a second on those in opposition. Their messages will be tailored to those of us most likely to take action.

We need the old heads to temper those youthful messages with their own brand of wisdom. They know that knowledge comes from books. That is a centuries-old maxim that we used to great advantage during Civil War III.

Black protest literature burned our eyes and enflamed our hearts – 'Manchild in the Promised Land,' 'The Autobiography of Malcolm X,' 'Letters from a Birmingham Jail,' 'For Colored Girls Who Have Considered Suicide, When the Rainbow is Enuf' – all created moments that changed our turbulent American history.

In those moments, we recognized the history of lying and cheating they foisted upon us. We disparate tribespeople became one tribe. Though privation and lawlessness were forced upon us, we became a family through those horrors. We reveled in our power to survive subhuman conditions that we never deserved.

That is what our system of ascendance should draw on and emulate. Whether it is six websites or 6,000; one book or dozens, to succeed we need to make each project a pathway to our ultimate goal. Our projects require firm milestones and deadlines, or else they're just dreams. We should aim for that ultimate goal with every tool at our disposal.

We may even surpass our Jewish-Mexican template because their cohesiveness was forged in a pre-iPad 20th century that used traditional methods of communication. The Jewish struggle for acceptance dates back to the biblical era. It was slow, painful and, as in our own Middle Passage era, millions of lives were snuffed out by the enemy.

A solely book-based campaign would slow our progress. Success will spring from a melding of generational ideas and technologies.

One of the greatest things in our favor is evolution. Concepts, once realized, evolve. Google's iconic opening page is clean and simple because co-founders Larry Page and Sergey Brin couldn't write HTML code.

Google has evolved into the world's most popular search engine, but that runt of a page has retained basically the same look despite the fact that Brin and Page could hire an army of programmers to redesign it. The face looks the same, but the body is something altogether different.

Our own evolution should be similar. Outwardly, we will look the same, but the face of the neighborhood hype will morph into that of the local bank president. The former playground basketball star mowing grass for a living will be a biological engineer.

Expect Resistance

Any attacks on the concept will primarily be from within our community. We are heterogeneous in most things, so we will speak with many voices. Forces outside our community will not be as powerful in their obstruction because we are asking a very basic question: 'What is the best way to get the message out?'

Determining the communication process is a decision so internal that our opponents would have to be from within the community to see the importance. That is precisely where they will spring from. They are the spiritual descendants of the colonial paper suppliers who refused to provide blank pages for the Declaration of Independence.

Their Resistance, Our Response

Our opponents are doomed to failure because once the process starts, black focus is amazing. The end goal is almost immediately reified by our collective efforts. Consider the Civil Rights Movement. With no army, few weapons and no political heft, we bent the will of the most powerful nation on Earth. That is an indication of the black community's power. It hasn't gone away, despite the best efforts of the Sons of the South. But, it has fallen into disuse.

Set in motion, the process will attract elite achievers and visionaries. Action will unleash the strongest of us and what was once our dysfunction will become a powerful weapon – strong individuals taking action. Our negative members will be washed away by a stream of successes that propel the model further.

Once the ball is rolling, it will be advisable to recognize the progress toward these goals – or whatever these goals mutate into. True believers should recommend ways to achieve them and feel comfortable in doing so. Tearing down others' ideas or insisting there is only one correct method is counterproductive.

Our ultimate success in unleashing this new age relies on a cooperative core of people. Too much attention paid to detractors is wasted time and energy. Our goal should be to rearrange the words of this book into a real-world change engine, a new, black-focused economy

That change engine should have clearly defined goals that address our collective challenges in finance, education, housing, employment and social power.

Chapter 10
Money is a Means, Not "The End"

I don't know what, they want from me/It's like the more money we come across/The more problems we see –
'Mo' Money, Mo' Problems,' – Notorious B.I.G., ft. Mase & Puff Daddy

Money. Some people got to have it. Some people really need it. That 'mean green' the O'Jays sing about might seem like a major character in this book. It's not.

America is addicted to money. We pay money for oxygen bars, virtual land and weapons in video games. We pay to park our cars and pay more if we park them too long. We pay sundry fines. We pay to be at the front of the line.

But, this book, as it invokes capitalism, collective financial achievement, housing, jobs and other financial matters, is well aware that money is not what's ultimately important. Time is the most precious of any human's possessions. That is easily forgotten because we have transformed it into a commodity through the use of cash. We believe we can conquer time with money; we hire maids to help us save time from cleaning. We hire workers to expand the time we can use to generate dollars.

In America, not talking about money is an oddity. One can survive without it – literally – but that existence is a markedly different one than 99.9 percent of Americans. It's the kind of lifestyle on which news outlets do incredulous stories.

In our lifetime, money has won the culture war. It owns the courts, the politicians and the police. Things that used to be free – water! – now cost us. We are so conditioned to open our wallets and pay that one of the scam artist's most lucrative cons is simply sending a bill to a mark. Many of us pay, assuming it's a bill we overlooked.

That is a learned response that owes much to Madison Avenue.

So, this book offers methods to assure our collective financial security, leave money to the next generation, create millionaires and billionaires and set up lucrative industries.

But, the goals of a truly empowered black civilization are education, power, equality, opportunity and social growth. Money is a means to an end. It can be a confusing balancing act. Rappers, daily, tip over into a grotesque, greenbacks idolatry. Many of them happily announce that "cheddar" is more important than a human life and they're willing to shoot somebody to prove it.

'Mind on my money,' indeed.

But, don't allow white America's affection for rap to dictate a black reality: rap is a reflection of our youth culture. It is the cry of our young men and women trying to find their way in a society that seems to hate and fear them. Of course, they fixate on money – money facilitates American life.

This isn't a slam on rap and its culture; young kids, in general, are supposed to be callow. Wisdom comes with failures and the realization of empathy. It is a human condition for our children to struggle for their place in the world.

Rappers grew up in an America that has drifted so far into the money mindset that even adults don't know the definition of free. Companies that give us something extra when we pay or provide them with our personal information are not giving us anything free. They are giving us a discount. Yet, we're so accustomed to paying we don't dispute the use of "free."

The late Wallace "Hotada" Francis, a cultural minister with the original Black Panthers, spent a lifetime discussing this illusion. He was well aware of our capitalist system's false offers, but always took it to a deeper level.

"You're not free," he would say to the young wisdom-seekers at his knee. "You're loose."

He would lament a youth culture that writes songs about Cristal, Maybachs and iced wrists at the exclusion of family and an uplift of their culture. Still, he understood the process. The American music industry, like any big business, distills an essence and sells it without regard to societal niceties. We have been sugared, salted, technologized and armed to the teeth. And, we are taught to desire – with every fiber of our being – the next thing money can buy. Money, meanwhile, is simply the shadow of all of those desires, the sine qua non that makes it all happen.

Our distractions are infinitely more sophisticated than those of our forebears. We are the greatest consumers of entertainment in history. If America's leaders tried to force any of us, black or white, to a literal place of bread and circuses, the riots would be spectacular.

Youth are impressionable and rap has created millions of white acolytes echoing black youth culture because it has made it onto the established channels.

But, black culture is not solely youth culture; it is not even mostly youth culture. Youthful passion must have an outlet and evolve into something more stable and less self-centered. Tupac and Biggie are the end results of a youth-only black culture. It can't survive past the 20s or 30s. A 50-year-old man shooting people for stepping on his shoes, getting high every night or slanging for a living is a failure in his family and in his community.

That's not an indictment of our youth culture. The young of every culture must make their mistakes and act out on their existential anger. It is part of the progression to adulthood.

Retarding or destroying that progression leads to gang bangers shooting babies to death to make a point in a low-level drug deal. Such evil isn't even restricted to humans – studies suggest that taking away the adult males from a group of elephants leads to teen-aged male elephants that are aggressive, violent and self-destructive.

Black culture was willfully fragmented by white society, but our ancestors weren't eradicated, despite American society's best efforts. At this late date, to enter into a new phase and truly believe wealth accumulation is the primary reason for existence ties us into that dynamic, but stunted youth culture.

It's easy to be confused by the madly mixed signals presented to us by the nation we helped build. Ironies abound: many of us argue in favor of labor unions against conservatives, but unions perpetrated some of the worst racism against us in the industrialized north. We defend the aims of the federal government, especially in the age of Obama, despite the facts of the Tuskegee Experiment, federally approved housing discrimination and more. We decry the use of guns with the uneasy knowledge that non-violence alone didn't keep us alive in the South in the 1950s. Our grandfathers' rifles helped a lot.

We need to see much more clearly how majestic our future, the apex of our 10,000-year pageant, can be. We easily live with the ironies because of the dual consciousness we possess, the combined consciousness W.E.B. DuBois and Frantz Fanon separately chronicled as a survival technique. Irony is easy; what we can't live with is a future without a plan.

White America has profited from a systemic plan designed to benefit them. Many of them know which grade schools lead to great careers – it is a system with a plan. Many have slots waiting for them at prestigious universities – it is a system with a plan. After graduation, a network of Moose, Elk, Masons and Daddy's Buddies assure their career paths.

It is a system. With a plan.

They buy their insurance from friends of the family – it is a system, with a plan. Their homes are paid for with down-payments funded by lifelong jobs.

It is a system. With a plan.

It is not inadvertent. It may seem like good luck, but white people are very good at making monetary systems that benefit them. They are even better at excluding those they choose to exclude.

Anyone with a sense of history knew what was coming in 2009, when President Obama was elected to deal with the mess of an historic financial meltdown. Black unemployment rates shot up, the black middle class shrank, mainstream banks refused to lend to us and hundreds of thousands of us lost our homes to foreclosure.

And, we were blamed for it. Everything.

They said we broke the system.

The President served as our proxy and racists and Republicans showed the world their dishonesty, laziness and true disregard for America.

The same people who, a few years earlier, shouted down liberals angry with George W. Bush, labeling them traitors to America, were now doing much worse – and calling it patriotism. 'My country 'tis of thee – unless a black man is in the Oval Office.'

Black history is full of murdered patriots. We never had a true advocate at the highest levels of power, but we still believed in this country. Contrast that with white people who were "patriots" until racism trumped that sentiment.

Patriotism has done us few favors. It didn't stop the lynchings of brave black American soldiers. President Obama's election and re-election forced millions of those false patriots, whiny, self-serving white Americans, into the open.

Black people bled and believed; these white people were inconvenienced and lost faith. A million or more of them around the U.S. wanted to secede from the Union because of the election. Like much of American history, it's certain that black citizens weren't consulted on those decisions.

Still, we are the staunchest patriots this country has ever seen. Our allegiance wasn't purchased like some Blackwater security contract; it was freely given. We didn't talk secession when the economy went bad for us or a racist was elected to office – which happened frequently. But, let's separate our system of governance from our economic system. Democracy is not the same as capitalism.

If we believe our betterment is only about making more money, our cause is in trouble. Black people should have much more money because that's what America does – it rewards with cash. It has rewarded dozens of reasonably intelligent white people in the tech industry with billionaire status. It's enriched the inventors of the pet rock, the smiley face and Post-It note. What is insane is that many people of all races believe there is something inherent in the black psyche that prevents our success. We couldn't put a rock in a box, draw a circle, two dots and a semi-circle or stick some glue on the back of a little yellow piece of paper? Really?

There is no individual deficiency in black people. The reality is we are being pummeled because we underestimate the power of white supremacy in America. It is not a force of nature we are fighting. We fight a consortium of flesh-and-blood white people who exclude us with regularity.

'We'd love to hire black people – in tech, rocket science, advertising, you name it – but, we can't find a qualified candidate,' they say. It is the lie of meritocracy, which ironically, we are the last ones in America to fully believe. There is precious little meritocracy in American capitalism. The lower economic rungs are filled with brown faces who will work for minimum wage; the upper economic rungs are filled with golf buddies and legacy Yale graduates.

Black people make it so much easier for these liars by not planning a collective response. There is a proverb about a lie racing halfway around the world before the truth can tie its shoes. We need to catch up.

It gets back to youth culture; it is a culture that is of the present moment. It 'plans' to get high, have sex and flip the middle finger to old people.

Certainly, there are strains of wisdom in youth culture. Youthful hope transforms to action and obstacles crumble. The leaders of the American Colonies were young people; the Civil Rights Movement Warriors were often children. Society needs youthful energy to work in concert with experience.

But, rap culture, aside from some conscious strains – PM Dawn, Nas, Mos Def, Taleb Kweli, The Roots and some bits and pieces of 'gangsta' – isn't constructive. It casts white society as a backdrop against which black culture is to blame. The people it targets to shoot in its songs? Young black men. The women it degrades with profanity? Young black women.

It is a sordid place to be for a proud people – being blamed by our children for economic inequities we didn't create. Still, they have a point. We may not have created most of the problems, but we damn sure could have better shielded our children.

If the collective black response to rap artists' cries had been, 'Yes! We aren't doing enough to protect our youth. We've got to get our shit together!' Then, their messages would have circumvented the white infrastructure that brings rap into our homes. It would have been revolutionary and we would have fomented a new Civil Rights Movement. That didn't happen.

The rap revolution stalled, but our culture should still heed the coded messages. If we don't organize – soon – this second-class citizenship will continue for generations and generations, forcing our descendants to do what their great-grandparents should have done – stand up, decisively, to power. If we continue the path we are on, history will record that black elders heard the sobbing of their young people and did nothing. Societies can't sustain themselves by cutting off their futures.

Money is a means, but until we rebuild our middle class, shore up our poor and force our upper-class to lead responsibly, it will always be a fleeting thing.

Chapter 11
Racists Want You to 'Go It Alone'

Some of the things that you just don't figure/'Cuz it gets a lot Blacker and a whole lot bigger/No matter, nightstick or bring your big trigger/Our nation is protected by some pro-Black niggas! –
'Fire & Earth,' X Clan

One of the most well-worn tools of modern racists is ascribing all of the world's racism solely to black people. As Hotada Francis often said, "I'd believe 'em if I ever saw a black man stop a white man from getting a job, a house or a car."

This book will be considered racist by many white people and most white people in the South. They will insist black people are inherently racist – as if slavery, lynchings, Jim Crow and financial redlining were mass hallucinations.

'Look at how you voted for the President, you elected him just because he was black,' those racists say with a sneer.

That idiocy ignores the thousands of white politicians black people voted for over the years and the fact that virtually identical percentages of black people and Southern whites voted for their presidential candidate of choice in 2008 and 2012. Ninety percent of black people voted for President Obama and 90 percent of white Southerners voted for whoever he ran against.

This is a common white supremacist argument: 'Our 90 percent support is reasoned and considered and colorblind. Yours is ignorant and racist.' Many have the nerve to describe black Democratic voters as having a 'plantation mentality.'

That is an insult to our ancestors and our intelligence. People who wish to keep black people shackled describe the Republican Party as the community's best friend. Apparently, our 'best friend' wants to control our vote by slamming our culture, attacking our leaders and calling us stupid.

With friends like that…

Democrats are far from perfect, but this is about as true a fact as American politics will allow: Republicans will not elect a black person as president and they certainly will not enact pro-black policies. Again, this is in keeping with certain white people's racist behavior. They have no problem with pro-Christian, pro-Southern or pro-white policies.

Those policies are antithetical to most pro-black policies, so all that's left for the GOP black recruitment troops is to lie about their intentions – lies that only 10 percent of us believe

Your vote is coveted as part of a Republican strategy that seeks the diminution of Democratic power. If a 10 percent black vote total keeps the GOP candidate out of office, they will do all they can to ensure a nine percent black vote total.

One of the most amusing things about both Obama victories was after their losses, when hundreds of Republicans offered a very specific remedy for expanding the GOP electorate: white women, Hispanics and Asians were repeatedly said to be crucial to their future. Notice any group missing? The second largest racial group in America – black people.

Twenty-first century racism is alive and unapologetic. The late former presidential candidate George McGovern said it well in a paper he wrote on progressive politics. He said those who consider themselves revolutionaries don't play by the rules, so a lie to your enemy is not only acceptable, it is desired. They take pride in lying to black people.

White reactionaries fear an America full of powerful black people and will say whatever they must to prevent that future.

Our electoral efforts, resulting in the election of some black officials, aren't racist. Never believe anyone whose mouth forms that lie. Even if you do vote by skin color, you are making a vote in your self-interest, something every white subgroup takes for granted and they are never called on that self-interest. We want black politicians not because we're homogenous or race-focused, it's because so many white people have proven time and again they will not fully consider our collective interests. It doesn't matter the politician – either Clinton, FDR, JFK – we are sold out easily and without qualm. We vote for black politicians to protect ourselves from indifferent white pols.

It is not racist to defend yourself, despite the verdict in the Trayvon Martin murder case.

In the 21st century and beyond, black Americans must seize the courage of their forebears and speak the truth. Bigots are trying to hide racism under a billion fallen leaves. They point to black-on-black crime, while ignoring white-on-white crime; they call Affirmative Action racist because it allows hires of the unqualified despite having no knowledge of the qualifications necessary. They speak in dog whistles and smoke vapors with the central aim of continued oppression.

'Above all,' they say in whispers: 'Don't let them organize!'

It is the black person's burden in America. We are discouraged from organizing to pursue a collective goal. Mothers mad at drunk drivers can organize. Gays and lesbians can organize. Bicyclists and environmentalists can organize. But, when the multiracial and conservative NAACP is mentioned in a news story, invariably some white person will inevitably opine, 'Where is *my* National Association for the Advancement of White People?'

They will follow that with, 'When are *we* going to have a White History Month?'

In their perverted world view, we are not allowed to question racist intent, speech or behavior, because they are 'tired of it.' Our response? 'If you're tired, take a nap, because this thing is only going to get bigger.'

Because their prejudices are so profound, they're unable to see this book as a godsend for their oft-stated complaints. It offers a way for the black community to empower itself – no need for a Great White Father's intervention.

At least, that would be their reaction if they were telling the truth about their hatreds. They say black people need to improve their own community, but if that really happened, it would be catastrophic for them.

The mid-21st century and beyond will be a time of black bosses, major media owners, landlords, presidents, doctors, tech geniuses, governors and a million other decision-makers. It will be a truly ugly meritocracy for those haters because they will finally have to work for their supper instead of being shuttled to the front of the line by virtue of skin color.

It will be difficult for some of us to disregard catcalls of racism. Many of us fear how we are viewed in groups by white people. It was a problem during the Civil Rights Movement. 'Mister Charlie will be so disappointed in me,' some black people cried. 'He's been so good to me.'

That kind of thinking was shored up by the belief that if we just ignore the second-class treatment and act nice, things will eventually change. We all occasionally think that way because we inherited broad shoulders to accept more suffering. It is a remnant of slavery. Millions of us struggle in silence and refuse real help. Racists depict us as 'welfare queens' when every black person in America knows a dozens of people and families that have never accepted a dime of aid.

And, if the helping hand is black, centuries of brainwashing impute ulterior motives or inferior aid.

We are a people of, "I'll just do it my damn self."

That is not a true option, though some white people will swear black people should prosper solely as individuals. They say that because they know American history. America has an awful expertise at limiting the number of financially successful black people. They have always relied on a battle plan of outnumbering and outgunning black people. During that time in American history when black people outnumbered white people in some Southern states, they relied heavily on keeping that Census information away from black people so our ancestors never realized their numbers advantage. It is simple logic: one can't overcome many.

But, don't extrapolate too far. Though one can't defeat the many; the few in number absolutely can defeat a numerically superior enemy.

Racists don't stand a chance of preventing a collective black ascendance and they know it. The numbers game is no longer in their favor. Yes, there are more white people than black, but centuries of oppression have bonded black people more solidly than white people. That is a unique strength that fractured white society can't hope to duplicate as a whole – not when white Christians hate white Muslims and white gays and white liberals and white Northerners.

Our collective empathy is stronger, and not just because we donate more of our time and money to charity than white people. We have been targeted by centuries of cruelty; we are students of cruelty because we either have endured or individually know the tortures of which the larger group is capable.

When innocents are murdered and justice winks and laughs, a sympathetic bond is formed. Emmett Till was only related to a handful of people but he became a symbol that sparked the Civil Rights Movement. Virtually every black person in America can tell a Till-like tale of racial horror experienced by family. Uncles were tied to railroad tracks, mothers were raped, fathers were beaten. It makes an impression. Those injustices contribute to our capacity for empathy. It crosses the boundaries that separate us – skin color, money, geography because of our empathy.

There are extremely wealthy black people in America who give back to people they could easily ignore. Our middle class was decimated, but there still exists a smaller middle class that does what it can for those in need. The bond exists – for most of us – despite social class.

Part of the reason for that cross-class bond is that white people at every class level are afforded extra privileges; black backs are still being stepped on. Our social mobility is intentionally limited. For example, professional sports might look like an equalizer, but it would take 1,000 NBAs and NFLs to create the community-wide wealth enjoyed by white physicians. It is much easier to earn an MD degree than a $40 million contract in the NBA. Black people encounter an incredibly high bar when it comes to earning equitable pay.

In a 25-year study of black and white low-income people in Baltimore, published by the Russell Sage Foundation, the white poor benefited from a lifetime of hidden perks because of their race. White men endured shorter periods of unemployment, were more likely to work full-time, in the industrial/construction trades, and earned exactly twice as much – $43,000 to $21,500 – as black workers and 84% without high school diplomas were employed, compared to 40% of black people.

According to a 2011 Pew Research Center study, middle-class white people possessed $111,000 in median net worth compared to $33,500 for middle-class black people. White middle-class Americans possess "between three and five times as much wealth as equally achieving black middle-class families."

Researchers Melvin Oliver and Thomas Shapiro write: "Black [people's] claim to middle-class status is based on income, not assets... without wealth reserves, especially liquid assets, the black middle class depends on income for its standard of living." An over-reliance on income explains the devastation the Great Recession wreaked on the black middle class – dropping millions of black Americans into the struggling class.

And, at the very highest levels of income – billionaires – the numbers bear out America's racial exclusion. Despite being 14% of the population, only three black Americans are billionaires: Oprah,

Michael Jordan and maybe Dr. Dre, who represent filmed entertainment, sports and music. At this writing, there are 492 US billionaires, meaning 0.61% America's billionaires – about half of one percent – are black.

It's a different picture when discussing Jewish wealth at the highest level. Though Jewish people comprise only two percent of America's population, they make up 40% of America's billionaires. And, most of the Jewish middle-class is employed in the three highest paying job sectors: professional/technical, management/executive and business/finance.

It is a very simple goal we have. We don't want to pull even with white America; we want to take the path of Jews – and gays and Asians – in America. Our goal is to soar above the average in wealth and income.

For too long, we have been victims of averaging. When America's unemployment rates hovered near 10 percent, we were allegedly all in the same boat. No. Our boat was leaking profusely. If you pulled out black unemployment from the total average, white unemployment rates went down by percentage points.

In the world of lies, damned lies and statistics, the statistics are certainly pulling their weight. Overall housing, unemployment or wealth numbers might show a tepid economy – until numbers for black people are separated. We are America's statistical dividend. Our intra-group numbers are so bad they pull down the average. That allows white people to look at each other from across their suburban streets and say, 'Hey! I'm not doing so badly!' while across town black families are being evicted.

To see what's happening to us, we have to be willing to look. That means a black-focused view. Just as it would be absurd to include male salaries as anything but comparison points in a study of female wage earners, it makes no sense to hide black data within white data when the disparities are so pronounced. Excluding data on men from a female study doesn't make it sexist, anymore than focusing on black improvement is racist.

With a simple, easily identified, black-focused goal – being above average on U.S. wealth indicators – we have clarity of purpose. Our best actions and strategies grow clearer.

Accusations of racism are meant to fog that purpose.

In the words of esteemed comedian Mr. Paul Mooney, "It's getting too late in the day for that bullshit."

Chapter 12
Random Acts of Blackness

Don't give up/and don't give in/although it seems/you never win –
'Optimistic,' Sounds of Blackness

Most of the suggestions in this book are formed, finished and implemented solely by the black community. This chapter has a different focus – it offers suggestions that require cooperation with other communities of people.

The first suggestion is about an American obsession – gambling. Gambling was one of the first underground economies created by black people denied legal means to support themselves and their families.

The Numbers

They called it 'the Numbers' and from Quincy, IL to Harlem, NY, it offered bits of hope to desperate people who saved their pennies for a chance at anything from ten dollars to thousands.

The numbers-runners made a good living and a few lucky souls were able to pay their bills for the month. But, the white community's number one rule still existed – leave nothing for black people. So, the obvious course of action for racists of the time was to steal it away. First, the Mafia – with cooperation from law enforcement – overran the game. Ellsworth Raymond "Bumpy" Johnson operated one of the largest numbers rackets in Harlem. He was besieged by gangsters who "collected taxes" on his operation. The dollars that once stayed in our community began to flow into white communities.

A generation or two later, after organized crime had grown wealthy through its gambling monopoly – among other illicit endeavors – the government took over. State lotteries were legalized and Powerball fever took hold.

It's true that gambling is a vice with the potential to destroy lives and it is not a method to uplift a community. In fact, it's a horrible wealth-building strategy. Still, it was a powerful symbol of hope snatched away from the community when any bit of hope was golden.

It is a symbol that could – and should – be fully returned to the black community. In its present form, the lottery primarily enriches white people. Its astronomical odds aren't racist, but the end result is greater benefits for those who have larger population numbers. Black winners of huge jackpots are vanishingly rare.

And, remember, it's only the gambling side of the equation that forces the masses to lose their money. On the administration side, families may be fed and futures bolstered from the proceeds. If a Powerball-like numbers game was instituted solely within the black community – members only – the dollars would be relatively smaller, but certainty would exist: black winners, black administrators, black money.

There are no official numbers, but given the pervasiveness of gambling in all communities, educated guesses would suggest overall black wealth would rise by a percentage point, or several.

A black-owned lottery wouldn't solve our community's financial issues, but it would help. Right now, gambling in America is a white person's blood sport. Like other large industries, it forces us into consumerism while the producers reap the benefits. It's time to end that monopoly.

Income Tax Moratorium

Moving from one form of revenue collection to another, the black community needs to change its relationship with the tax collecting arm of the U.S. government. If legitimate reparations for the generational harm of slavery aren't soon forthcoming, we need to whip the Congressional Black Caucus into a frenzy to support a tax holiday for black Americans.

It's the mildest form of redress for slavery – we get to keep more of the money we earn as a payoff for working centuries with no wages at all. Set a period of, say, 20 years, and allow all legally earned income of black workers to be exempt from state and federal income taxes.

We would still be hit hard by social security, sales, local income and myriad other taxes, but such an exemption would slightly unburden the majority of black citizens. Politicians would hate it, but, as nearly every American forgets, politicians are supposed to work for us. Considering how poorly black America has been represented, we are owed this exemption.

White resentment is a certainty. Remember, many want you to have nothing. But, their resentment, along with the resistance of white politicians, is irrelevant. Keeping 15 percent or 20 percent more of the money we earn won't come close to bridging the U.S. wealth gap, but, again, it's a start.

Some of the loudest voices protesting will be our own.

Black people who profess to hate singling out black citizens for a special privilege have learned nothing during their time in America. They are blind to systemic discrimination and many honestly believe that their personal successes can be achieved by all black people. They conveniently forget their math and history. Numerical minorities have always been favored in the 'divide and conquer' system.

It's a strategy based on variable reinforcement, one of the most powerful psychological motivators available.

An example of variable reinforcement is slot machine gambling. The odds in fair games are randomized, but if you win a jackpot wearing a blue shirt, that shirt then becomes your lucky blue shirt. We ascribe cause and relation to the shirt and payout, despite neither existing. It is a powerful motivator because we don't know when or *if* it will happen again. This is compared to continual reinforcement where we would receive jackpots on each play. We might get bored, lose the thrill and consider it a job. Or, negative reinforcement, where we never receive a jackpot, become frustrated and stop playing.

Social experimentation isn't quite so random, but random (variable) acts of reinforcement are there to view.

Allow extremely few black people into the schools, programs and companies of the upper class and you're seen as an inclusive white society. Dangle strings of wealth and advancement that only a small fraction of the favored minority will ever achieve and the narrative is shaped: they've created an erroneous belief that the remaining vast majority *must* share a common defect blocking their achievement. And, it's not too far a leap for them to suggest lower intelligence amongst black people.

White American legislators are well aware of this game, even if conservative black people are not. Every "pro-black" law ever written has possessed strings.

Every instance of supposed support for America's black citizens was tainted. Every act of redress contributed some harm. Welfare, for instance, provided subsistence-level existence, but forced black men out of their homes. Early voting rights legislation was thwarted by poll taxes and literacy tests. Affirmative Action was affirmative for the careers of white women, but, in large measure, only ensured that black men and women were interviewed for positions. Interviews don't pay the bills.

There is a belief among some of the black men who benefited from Affirmative Action that a seven-year window existed – from roughly 1964 to 1971 – and after that period racial Affirmative Action was closed for business.

The elections of President Obama were high water marks for U.S. racial relations, but don't forget black voters made the keenest difference. Millions of fair-minded white people voted for a black man, yes, but there were millions *more* white people in 2008 and 2012 who *didn't* vote for a black man.

Only a fool would attribute racism to each and every white vote against the President. But, based on Republican/conservative strategy after his elections, racism played a significant part.

Racism in a post-Obama world has the potential to be virulent and only slightly less obvious than what we have seen in the Obama years. The most cynical, politically-minded racists will hold up black political patsies like Herman Cain or Ben Carson with no serious intent of putting them in the White House.

What the typical black citizen needs to know is the Sons of the South and their sympathizers will try to make her the target of their anger for the Obama years. In the face of that anger, it will be our task to poke that bear. We need to channel the fearlessness of our grandparents and great-grandparents and fight institutional power with moral power.

We can't afford another generation of subservience; another century of 'not rocking the boat.' As white rapper Macklemore said, 'We've got to 'rock that motherfucker.'

If we are not at the table, we are on the menu. And, the Sons of the South are always famished for dark meat.

Just like Civil War II, the Sons of the South sense victory because millions of benighted white people have absorbed their spin and are blaming the President for his opponents' shortcomings in leadership. These men very clearly stated their goal years before the President's last day in office: they aim to erase his legacy. Obamacare? That's just the most obvious. They want to abolish Affirmative Action, family welfare, equal opportunity programs, Headstart, college admissions diversity – anything with a hint of black, and by association, Obama, in it.

They have already anointed Hispanics and gays as "the new black" and our "gift" was the 44th president of the USA. That was supposed to be our Affirmative Action, non-discrimination policy and jobs equalizer all in one.

If we accept that, we will be knocked back on our heels for the rest of the century. The President's election was a symbolic victory – but symbols are meaningless if not followed by action. That is why we must demand a federal and state tax moratorium.

At every level, black citizens, both powerful and powerless, will need to step up and say, "No income tax for us for 20 years."

After we declare it, after we achieve it, we must then implement our strategy. Why? Because, it won't be enough. Handouts aren't our future. After the law is passed, we must then take full advantage of it, setting our sights on a 20-year horizon filled with business development, community optimization and reconciliation, home ownership and succession planning.

Done right, tax emancipation means some future child, unborn at present, will marvel at the unusual financial state of 20th century black Americans. 'Poor black family' will be the same level of oxymoron as 'poor Jewish family.'

Consider this: why are government programs widely identified as helpful to the black community so poorly designed that they hurt as much as they help? Programs to help middle-class white people are sturdier: the USDA gutted black farmers, but its policies were an unqualified success in aiding most white farmers; most police departments are beloved by white citizens and feared by many black citizens; tax breaks on mortgages were amazingly successful, but most homeowners are white because black people were barred from bank home loans. The GI Bill, capital gains tax levels, the list of governmental discrimination goes on.

Even the most complex plans – Social Security, for instance – can be constructed well enough to provide the desired benefits. What sets apart social programs designed to help black people is the push and pull of legislation and racism. Legislators who view us as full citizens make an attempt to aid a struggling constituency – Sons of the South don't want that help offered, so they poison the process.

This law wouldn't have many moving parts; a black income tax moratorium is as simple as 'no.' No federal or state income taxes on black people for 20 years. White resentment will grow, but if they want to partake in the emancipation, all they have to do is prove they are black – and, many of them do have black ancestors. Easy.

It will be an amazing choice – Americans of other races will see a positive outcome from being black. Belonging to our community will offer a distinct, financial advantage. Oh, to be a fly on the wall of those white households when deciding whether to let the world know they have black blood.

And, we must not be deterred by the fact that we came up with this idea first. We should ignore the faux reasoning of those who offer, 'What about poor Appalachians?'

We have grown accustomed to being lumped in – with gays, Hispanics, white women, the differently-abled – and, often, those groupings send us to the back of the line. But, other groups are not diluted when it comes to reparations.

Native Americans were granted casino – gambling! – privileges, not Appalachians; Asian Americans detained in World War II were paid cash, no payouts were made to Germans; America was instrumental in creating a nation for Jewish people, not protestants, by confiscating land from Arabs and when our government championed a nation in Africa – Liberia – for freed slaves, they didn't send Chinese Americans to Africa.

We have traveled down a long, hazardous road with intentionally poor signage. It's time to return to a path that's positive for us. Luckily, what is good for black America is generally good for America as a whole. Our fight for civil rights alone has empowered a host of white demographic groups and strengthened our nation, but we have been locked out of full access to the American economy as if it were a child-proofed videogame.

That analogy fits the paternalism to which many white people subscribe.

"I believe in white supremacy, until the blacks are educated to a point of responsibility," film actor John Wayne said in a 1971 Playboy article. "I don't believe [in] giving authority and positions of leadership and judgment to irresponsible people."

Every single one of us has tired, at least once, of white people like John Wayne deciding our collective personality for us. It is the crap that we have to deal with – the White Man's Burden, plus a little extra. We can't visually blend in to white society like gay people; we don't have another nation to return to like immigrant Hispanics; we don't have the broad base of money and influence that Jews have.

We have to be tough because we are alone in this. We are asking other human beings to relinquish some of their social privileges for no other reason than it's the right thing to do. Black conservatives know that is a losing argument; they don't believe in appeals to the better nature of white people.

Our Civil Rights' victories put us on a shining path that was subverted by the Sons of the South. We made a wrong turn by underestimating the depth of their racism and its contagiousness.

The suggestions of this chapter are small steps toward equalization. Conservatives are fond of saying, 'Equal opportunity, not equal outcomes,' to justify their beliefs. Most black people would heartily agree, except for the fact we know the game is rigged. In our reality, the Washington Generals are kicking the Globetrotters' asses night in and night out. Something is wrong with that picture.

We say, 'Give us truly equal opportunity and you'll see the outcomes.'

Media Ratings

One of the easiest ways to cleanse the psychic damage visited on us, minute-by-minute, by media is a ratings system for all non-black media products: movies, still marketing photos, television programs, commercials, video games, newspapers, etc.

This will drive Hollywood insane, but that's a side benefit. This is a future-facing strategy. Those of us born in the 1900s and early 21st century are setting a better stage for our children born closer to the mid-21st century if we clearly mark the media that is bad for us.

Those of us with a foot in the 20th century have already been imprinted by our media. We know what's not one of our 99 problems, where the beef is, what type of beauty is best, who to fear most, the futility of fighting white supremacy and, most of all, how to be the best consumers possible.

We have media to thank for that. Black women who slam rich black NBA and NFL players for gravitating to non-black women are well aware those players grew up watching "iCarly," "Lizzie McGuire," "The OC," "Friends" and seeing only one standard of beauty – white women.

From the blonde weathergirl on the early morning news to Gwen Stefani music videos to the busty blondes on their videogames, young black men are inundated with beauty standards that don't include black women. Is it so unusual to carry those images into their nightly dreams? How, then, can desire not follow? This is not an excuse; it is a psychological observation.

That should be the first, official, media warning – NBI, for 'no black images.' Then, shows like 'Friends,' 'Seinfeld' and 'Girls,' which are all set in a New York with virtually no black people, would be labeled for what they are: segregationist fantasies.

Another warning might be FF for 'financial futility.' Hollywood *loves* a poor black person. Way back in the 1970s, when Red Foxx starred in 'Sanford & Son,' black television characters were never allowed to move up from lower class.

Foxx' character always came up with ways to hustle more money. His son, Lamont, always shot them down so the pair never moved out their junkyard. Compare that to its white contemporary, 'The Beverly Hillbillies.' That hillbilly family got rich in the first episode and richer with every passing season.

Other black TV families were also not allowed to do better – 'Good Times,' 'What's Happenin'' and 'The Jeffersons.' Yes, the Jeffersons were wealthy, but the running gag was they could never break into that next level of wealth. The subliminal message, for black people, is, 'Stay in your place.'

The warnings can be what we want them to be: 'BGDF' – black guy dies first, 'T' - token representation, 'SBGF' – sassy black girlfriend stereotype, 'BHR' – black history revision, GWPF - God-like White People Fantasies, for the countless superhero sagas, and so on.

What is important is that we label white-created media to warn of its negative effects on our minds.

It's not a foreign concept. In the latter 20th century, we marked everything, like Post-It notes in a Gabriel Garcia-Marquez novel. Sodium, sugar, calories, trans-fat, mattresses, albums, DVDs, videogames, you name it and there were parental warnings, sodium contents and fat percentages posted on our products and services.

This "third-party defining" supplanted our common sense and became the final arbiter for many of us in defining what was best or healthy. By being an audience to a century's worth of media created by people who either hated us or were indifferent to us, we are fluent in self-hate.

If our forebears hadn't stood taller than they were allowed, racist movies like 'Birth of a Nation' would be considered the epitome of art in its depiction of post-Reconstruction black terrorism. Some white people still do consider it one of America's finest films, as if the degradation of millions of people was somehow secondary to new camera angles.

Abdicating responsibility for defining what is good and bad can lead one down a dark path. There are strong arguments it already has. But, in an American consumer state with literally millions of product and service choices, the benefits of unbiased, accurate definition is obvious. No one has time to interview the farmer who provided his milk and eggs to ensure they are safe to eat. We trust because we must.

In defining healthy media for ourselves, we would take on a governing role without the authority of office. We have to assume the attitude of another group of warriors, Mothers Against Drunk Driving, or MADD, and foment an unwavering insistence on change.

More Black Doctors

One of our first global community partners should be any nation that partners with black America to send 20,000 young black students to medical school. Yes, it's an audacious goal to have so many at once and the infrastructure would creep close to overload in handling so many students and the costs would be in the range of sending a lunar module to Tranquility Base. And, yes, we would have to figure a way to deal with archaic residency requirements. Still it's a good, first-phase fix for the problem of blocking black people out of the hard sciences.

It's a different kind of doctor, but astrophysicist Neil deGrasse Tyson's social struggles in his virtually all-white field serve as an example. A February 2014 profile in The New Yorker magazine chronicled the soft racism of scientific exclusion:

> "Not long ago, Tyson's elementary school, P.S. 81, invited him to give a commencement address; he declined. He recalls telling the administrators, "I am where I am not because of what happened in school but in spite of it, and that is probably not what you want me to say. Call me back, and I will address your teachers and give them a piece of my mind."

> …

> "At the age of eleven, Tyson spoke with a teacher at P.S. 81 about his fascination with astronomy. Tyson's older brother, Stephen, who is an artist, recalls, "The teacher asked, 'Why do you want to go into science? There aren't any Negroes in that field. Why don't you go into sports?' " One evening, when he and his father were entering Van Cortlandt Park carrying a

telescope, the police stopped them. "I guess they thought it was a bazooka," [his mother] Sunchita says. "Just keeping my kids on the straight and narrow — and getting them not to hate people, in some instances, because of the way they were treated — was a full-time job." On another occasion, police were called to Tyson's building by neighbors who were alarmed by his rooftop activities; Tyson ended up showing the officers the stars."

…

"In a memoir, "The Sky Is Not the Limit," published in 2004, Tyson mentions that Caroline Kennedy was a classmate, but says that he had little time for social life: he was consumed by his studies, and he also joined the wrestling team. He often tells the story of how another African American member of the team, Frederick T. Smith—an eventual Rhodes Scholar, who intended to put his economics degree to use among impoverished communities—criticized him for devoting himself to science. 'Blacks in America do not have the luxury of your intellectual talents being spent on astrophysics,' he told Tyson. … 'Never before had someone so casually, yet so succinctly, indicted my life's ambitions,' Tyson later wrote."

If nothing else, the fact that white society is zealously guarding entry into the STEM disciplines suggests we should spend more energy trying to get into those disciplines.

There are about 850,000 medical doctors in 2014 America and an overwhelming majority of them are white. Adding 15,000 to that total – taking dropout rates into account – in the eight years' time it takes to become a practicing physician would barely move the needle. But, if you keep those 15,000 docs in the black community, it's a start.

Counting the 850,000 doctors for a population of 330 million, 0.26% of Americans are physicians – about a quarter of one percent. If every single one of the new doctors practiced exclusively in the black community, the percentage compared to white doctors serving the white community would still be worse. With 15,000 black doctors serving the black community, the percentage of physicians serving the black community would be 0.03%, eight times smaller.

That's how far educational roadblocks have set us behind in the high income professions.

Still, 20,000 medical students? How does a community make this kind of miracle happen? Good question. The cost would be in the billions between tuition, infrastructure, instructor salaries and other related costs. And, the payoff would be almost a decade away. So, a bank loan is out of the question.

But, for a people that won Civil War III without firing a shot, the impossible is just another rung on the ladder. The costs could be absorbed by government subsidies – and not necessarily U.S. subsidies.

If Cuba's leaders decided to train doctors – as it did for a number of nations when its health care system was subsidized by the former Soviet Union – it might bear part of the cost for political considerations from the U.S. government. Perhaps a partner could be found in Alika Dangote, Africa's $20 billion man.

Or, the black community could take a page from India's book and fund its own version of the Indian Institute of Technology for medical education and specifically for black students. The destination is obvious; the path chosen requires a burst of collective wisdom.

What will be glorious is an American with 15,000 highly educated physicians dedicated to a community mostly ignored by the medical profession. Health outcomes will improve, average life expectancy for black citizens will rise and persistent issues – high blood pressure, prostate cancer, breast cancer – will be addressed and minimized.

The financial impact will dwarf the cost. Fifteen thousand physicians making six-figure salaries, even if they're only 0.03 percent of the black population, will mean billions of dollars in wealth. It would have a larger impact than that of all the black professional athletes combined, because a running back has about a five-year shelf life; a physician can work for decades.

Chapter 13
Realities of Capitalism

Shawty/I don't mind if you dance on a pole/That don't make you a ho -
– 'I Don't Mind,' Usher

Capitalism is a system with sharp teeth and elbows. It creates competition for resources and markets and it is a terrible system of governance because it exploits those who are less powerful or unable to play the game.

Capitalism needs a scapegoat. It requires poorly compensated labor and cheap resources to grow larger. Slave labor was the gold standard for capitalism. It cut costs; it created a permanent underclass and it kept an entire class of competitors out of the system. Sons of the South are still smarting at having to compete with black business owners, which is why they spend so much time pushing the refresh button on racism in society.

In 1944, the Swedish economist Gunnar Myrdal found what he called an "American dilemma." He noted a huge chasm between American ideals of liberty and equality and the realities of African American life. Myrdal cited racism as the root of the problem because in interview after interview with white Americans, their support for segregation stemmed from believing black Americans were inferior.

Myrdal wrote that something had to give way, either white American attitudes had to change or the expectations of African Americans.

Because of the Civil Rights Movement, white American attitudes did change, but a full seat at the economic table has still not occurred in the 60 years since Myrdal's study. Capitalism is complex. Succeeding at the game of money requires a fluid intelligence coupled with extensive experience. The intelligence of the black community is above reproach; geniuses abound. We fall short on the second portion of the equation: experience in high finance.

There are a handful of black men and women who thrive in that rarefied air. But, without a Jewish kind of collectivism, they will not pull enough of the community far enough and fast enough to face the juggernaut that is coming our way.

That juggernaut, according to French economist Thomas Piketty, is a wealth inequity that is reverting global society back to 19th century levels, a time when robber barons bent national governments to their will, young children labored and died in factories and destitute people were jailed for the crime of being poor.

Piketty's book, "Capital in the 21st Century," studies wealth in capitalist societies around the world, all the way back to the 17th century. One of his central conclusions is wealth, except for the time period from 1913 to 1950, has always concentrated in the hands of the very wealthy because the rate of return on capital is higher than the rate of economic growth. It amounts to a nearly insurmountable economic head start for those born into wealth.

Put another, very narrow, way, it means those who work for a living and rely on an income cannot keep financial pace with those who possess capital such as land, buildings, natural resources holdings and other investments.

The money made from capital investment grows exponentially faster than the earnings from labor. And, if you look at the black community's finances, you will see we are not investors.

This complex game of capital has us playing 1940s style barnstormer basketball in a 21st century NBA setting. We are decades behind because of direct and purposeful obstructions attributable to slavery, Jim Crow and government complicity in systemic discrimination.

We have experienced generational setback after setback and are now expected to keep pace because America elected a black man as president. A logical rejoinder would be, 'No Jewish person has ever been elected president, but they seem to be doing well.'

If we view our situation for what it is – we are being obstructed in a million ways in part because of race and in part because capitalism needs a scapegoat/free labor – then we can begin to see how much we need each other to overcome that obstacle.

And, we don't even have to like each other to accomplish great things. Some of our richest white businessmen and most skilled white politicians hated their competitors, but managed to make both the American market and government work for their needs. That is a lesson for us. Crabs in a barrel are mindless arms and legs pulling down anything that crawls above them. We have never been crabs in a barrel; we have always been humans with a sense of reality, who knew that if white society allowed our neighbor more access, then our own access would be diminished.

Those were never our proudest moments, pulling down other black people, but given the centuries of privation and brutality, it makes sense in a context. That context must now be overwritten.

We must play the game of capitalism as well as we can because, unless another world war breaks out, the rich are about to get much, much richer, leaving the poor in some seriously dire straits.

"In all likelihood," writes Piketty, "the [wealth] gap will widen again in the 21st century as growth (especially demographic growth) slows … global growth is likely to be around 1.5 percent per year between 2050 and 2100, roughly the same rate as in the nineteenth century. The gap … would then return to a level comparable to that which existed in the Industrial Revolution."

Do a thought exercise. If there is no major change in strategy for black America, do you think the poorest of those late-century poor will be white or black? Capitalism evolves because its adherents desire its survival. The old reactions to bad capitalism don't work anymore.

Piketty cautions against assuming some nebulous forces of good will change the world and shrink the inequality. The most effective balancer of wealth between the very wealthy and the rest of the world has proven to be war. In World Wars I and II, capital losses from destruction of property, seized lands, losses of foreign assets, obliterated workforces and economies shrank the wealth gap and created the one time in recorded history that the economic growth rate grew larger than the rate of return on capital.

It's no coincidence that the white American middle class was created at the same time. No viable black middle class existed then because Jim Crow laws prevented equal access. We remained the nation's unskilled labor pool while poor, white, native-born Americans leaped further away from us in wealth and millions of Europeans arrived and lowered our meager earnings even more. Our relatively small and fragile middle class arose during Civil War III – the Civil Rights Movement.

Piketty's book offers little positive news to the struggling white American middle class. It congratulates them on their choice of being born during one of the most unusual economic periods in human history, but tells them the party is ending.

Like the barons of the 19th century, the Carnegies, Mellons, Astors and Rockefellers, the new rulers of capital, the Waltons, the Pages, the Ellisons, the Zuckerbergs et al, will own the nation and not feel any particular affinity for helping poor-by-comparison white strangers.

But, we are not white and that is our advantage. Understand this: many black and white people alike doubt the existence of a "black community" and, in small measure, they are right, just as they'd be right in saying there is no 'white male community.' Certainly, there are no meetings or memos to 45 million people. For black people, there is an historic commonality that overlays our American identity.

The vast majority of us have been mistreated and disrespected by citizens who have been given more rights than us because of skin color. If the centuries of discrimination hadn't happened, black skin might be a mere trait like blonde hair or green eyes. In light of our common history, our skin color connects us more than hair color connects blondes. There is a black America that is working to overcome discrimination.

Whiteness was created as a reaction to blackness. It was a marketing plan before the phrase meant anything. Back in the Middle Ages before the beginning of the slave trade, white and black people were just that – different colored people. In Shakespeare's time an interracial relationship, Othello and Desdemona, was unusual but not unlawful.

It's fascinating how far we have regressed as a species on that issue and even more fascinating that the descendants of slaves now have the power to join together for economic survival in ways white people cannot.

Think about it. There is no "white community." There are bands of racist white supremacists, certainly. But, their groups, Tea Party, LGBT organizations, fraternities and sororities, are ostensibly open to all.

The white community is a fissionable entity. Some will insist that 'America is a white community,' which is beyond absurd. Those white Americans often have a deep and abiding hatred for each other.

Italians, Irish and Jews once were not members of the pale club until someone looked around and realized that if these groups were considered black, then 'white' would be the minority.

That is our power. They define themselves in terms of our existence. It's as if we are the scorned mother in the film 'Imitation of Life' giving birth to a successful, ungrateful child who hates us, but owes us.

We need to use that power. Despite all of our differences, black people can collectivize much more easily than white people. Every suggestion in this book, every blueprint, would be virtually impossible for the 200 million white people of this nation. But, for the 45 million black citizens of America, these strategies are comparatively easy to implement.

Our situations are generally more dire. The white middle class is under siege, ours is nearly gone. They cut corners to maintain their lifestyles, while our lifestyles have been blown apart. Black homeowners became homeless; six-figure incomes vanished to nothing; retirement was put off until death.

We are motivated to change our lot. We are small enough to quickly effect lasting change and large enough to fight off our opponents.

And, like our previous battles for civil rights, we don't need an army or weapons. Give us what we didn't have before – a black-focused media, legal system and financial system and watch our dust.

We can't afford to wait for the snapback from the 'Obama haters' and we certainly can't afford to dig ourselves out of *another* economic hole. That would be criminal negligence on our part.

All the evidence indicts the Sons of the South's plans for another generation of black second-class citizenship.

Shame on us if we let that happen again.

Our warriors were caged, but they never stopped being warriors, just as a caged tiger never stops being a tiger. The blood of Harriet Tubman, Bro. El-Hajj Malik El-Shabazz, Toussaint l'Overture, Dr. Martin Luther King, Jr. and millions of other brave souls flows in our bodies.

We may not be free, but we are loose and we have the power to make ourselves free – if we choose.

Prisoner Reconciliation

Some in our community are literally not free. A million of our men and several thousand women are locked up as surely as their ancestors in the antebellum South. Most are locked up because of Ronald Reagan's 'War on Drugs.' If a similar proportion of prisoners existed for the entire U.S., we would have to imprison every man, woman and child of both Chicago and Los Angeles, with Minneapolis thrown in for balance.

Certainly, there are a great number of black prisoners in need of reminders that society requires civility – no killing, violence, robbery and other major crimes.

But, the drug trade grew out of two types of despair that could have easily been addressed if America's white leaders had the moral fiber to do so. One part of the despair was simply human reaction to constant beatdowns and social terrorism: drug abuse.

A certain proportion of all humans will seek out chemically-induced stupor to void out the sharp pains of existence; X, tequila, weed, heroin, crack and any new designer bath salt that pops up will make its way into their bodies with their full permission. The War on Drugs offered most of America's white citizens' treatment while at the same time jailing black citizens in wholesale fashion.

The second part of the despair was the horror of being unable to provide for oneself and one's family. This was particularly difficult, given America's patriarchal history, for black men who were forced to admit to hungry children and wives they could no longer feed, clothe or shelter them.

The drug trade, with all its ugliness and violence, was an expression of an oppressed people's desire to fend for themselves. It thrived because of rampant despair.

And, white people profited from it. Reporter Gary Webb, who died alone in a motel room under mysterious circumstances, wrote a series of articles that suggested the CIA flooded drugs into the black community to support clandestine war efforts.

The Italian Mafia and other criminal organizations made – and are making – billions of dollars selling drugs in the black community. A character in the 'Godfather' feature films bragged about dumping mind-altering poison in our community. The character was fictional; the statement was not.

By now, everyone knows the numbers. Black and white Americans use drugs at roughly the same rate. The differences lie in arrests and jail time. Black drugs users are about four times more likely to be arrested. After they are arrested, they're 20 times more likely to be sentenced to jail.

Behind bars, the rubber hits the road. In a nation still crawling out from under the legacy of slavery, would black people be able to avoid being treated as modern-slave slaves, despite misbehavior?

No. Black men and women are treated as chattel.

All prisons are guilty of this, but private, for-profit prisons are among the worst offenders.

Here is our action item. We need to demand of federal legislators that they make private prisons illegal in America. Warehousing human beings, black, white or brown, should at least be done solely by the state, as imperfect as that has been.

Companies like Correctional Corporation of America, CCA, and Wackenhut make billions by forcing men and women, mostly of color, into labor on behalf of for-profit companies. Prisoners are overcharged for better food choices, phone calls and toiletries and often can't buy these items with wages as low as 80 cents an hour.

These men and women are enslaved by the profit motives of others. They are pressured to work by prison guards, wardens pressure the guards and the prison administrators pressure the wardens.

CCA and Wackenhut control 75 percent of America's private prisons. Created during the Reagan administration, these companies receive a guaranteed amount of money for each prisoner, regardless of what it costs to maintain each prisoner.

Reporter Vicky Pelaez quoted private prison administrator Russell Boraas in an online article for El Diario-La Prensa.

"The secret to low operating costs," Boraas said, "is having a minimal number of guards for the maximum number of prisoners ... The CCA has an ultra-modern prison in Lawrenceville, Virginia, where five guards on dayshift and two at night watch over 750 prisoners. In these prisons, inmates may get their sentences reduced for 'good behavior,' but for any infraction, they get 30 days added – which means more profits for CCA."

Pelaez described the profits that motivate:

"The prison industry complex is one of the fastest-growing industries in the United States and its investors are on Wall Street. This multimillion-dollar industry has its own trade exhibitions, conventions, websites, and mail-order/Internet catalogs. It also has direct advertising campaigns, architecture companies, construction companies, investment houses on Wall Street, plumbing supply companies, food supply companies, armed security, and padded cells in a large variety of colors.

"According to the Left Business Observer, the federal prison industry produces 100 percent of all military helmets, ammunition belts, bullet-proof vests, ID tags, shirts, pants, tents, bags, and canteens. Along with war supplies, prison workers supply 98 percent of the entire market for equipment assembly services; 93 percent of paints and paintbrushes; 92 percent of stove assembly; 46 percent of body armor; 36 percent of home appliances; 30 percent of headphones/microphones/speakers; and 21 percent of office furniture."

Housing as many "prisoner/units" as possible and forcing them to work for far less than minimum wage is an obvious capitalist move. But, like the slaveowners of yesteryear, these businesspeople forget that these prisoner/units are people.

They are mothers, fathers, sons and daughters. When they die in private prisons – because of medical cost cuts – living, breathing families are devastated.

Private prisons are a relatively small portion of the Great American Incarceration of two million souls. But, even if they hold only 20,000 prisoners, their Sons of the South symbolism must be eradicated.

Believe in the Black Community

This book has mentioned the 'Crabs in a Barrel' mentality several times. Black people are no more prone to it than any other people – women are often chastised for not supporting women, as well – but our opportunities are so infrequent and remote that it seems worse when we pull down our own.

Part of it is an American distrust of authority. From Black Panthers to Tea Partiers, we don't trust the guy in the lead. And, because our institutions have generally been smaller and less financially robust, that reflects, wrongfully, on our capacity for leadership.

For the society-changing proposals in this book, indulging in that distrust is counterproductive. Those who choose to lead us on this path may be more intelligent, or not. They may be tactical geniuses, or not.

They are the right leaders because they take the chance to be in front of all those slings and arrows, both black and white. We followers need to have their backs so we can provide them with what the leaders of the Civil Rights Movement enjoyed: our collective genius and wisdom.

Our task is to maintain a connection that we aren't inclined to sabotage. To do so, means to attribute high value and worth to our own efforts. We can't hire white people to come in and clean up this historic mess of a racial climate – even though they are culpable. We can't reprogram their collective behavior.

We can't manage white people, we can only manage ourselves. Even The Database isn't a white person management tool, it's a detection instrument. What we do with the data it detects is always up to us.

Some of us need to stop hating each other and strategize. At this second, there are white men who would gladly kill each other in different settings, yet, they sit together in boardrooms and strategize. Some of our best young minds get homicidal over the color of a rag.

Get beyond that animosity and we will be able to further build up our existing black organizations so they may be retooled for grander purposes. Why waste time reinventing the wheel? It will take an intelligent community effort to bring about these changes. That is a prospect that makes the Sons of the South chortle.

Why? Again – many black and white people doubt the existence of a "black community."

We shall overcome. It's not just a song lyric. When we do, we need to realize that victory will not be a cure-all, anymore than our victory in Civil War III solved all our problems. There will still be suffering.

Some of us will still choose poorer outcomes. And, white people will be able to call out those who choose those poorer outcomes. We won't get every job we want. We won't be the subject of woe-is-us media coverage. Black women will probably continue to out-earn black men.

Some things will fall by the wayside. We will never be the underdog again. Real meritocracy is brutal; we either perform or step aside. Black dreams will be dashed along with white and we don't get to blame racism.

We won't be on financial par with the Jews at first. Our economic profile will more closely resemble white Gentiles. Even when we reach a Jewish level of economic success – a financial level-up – we need to remember not all Jews are rich.

This is the dream and it's not a delusion featuring golden sidewalks; it's us deciding our own fate from a position of power. The honeymoon will fade. We have to understand, upfront, it will only mean fewer hard days, not easy days. That's the curse of being human.

Our task is to make these changes without asking permission. Asking whites to give up privilege is like asking black people to give up Affirmative Action. Both groups hold on fast to their safety nets. Certainly, the analogy isn't perfect. Very, very few black people have directly benefited from Affirmative Action while white privilege gives a direct societal advantage.

Still, the change has to happen and the audience that needs to be convinced is black America: the 'I don't want to be bothered,' people, the 'I'm a conservative/libertarian,' people, the 'I'm doing fine,' people. For these groups and a hundred more groups of doubters, change agents must show hard evidence. .

We have to see with more than sight. We need data to prove to the doubters in our ranks – not their ranks – we have to stand up and make serious changes in our society.

There is a Somali proverb that goes: "Naftu orod bay kugu aamintaa." It translates to "Life in danger trusts only running" The message is simple: Run. Move.

Those who are standing still, holding on to a shaky status quo, risk being defined and marginalized by those in control of the system. A system doesn't care who controls it, anymore than a gun cares who shoots it. It's been amply demonstrated with our black President and Attorney General that the system doesn't break down because of the skin color of the officeholder. Our roadblocks have been created by angry white people – the Sons of the South.

They represent a clear and systematic deterrent to black control. But, their strength is their greatest weakness. Most of these men and women are obvious in their hatred and disdain for black people. That information allows the wise warrior to adjust her tactics. She can easily go around and, when necessary, through someone so irrational.

It's the strategy President Lyndon Johnson used to surprise the hell out of racist Democrats in the mid-1960s. The Dixiecrats possessed a Solid South in a nation that was still lynching black people. They felt invincible against the passage of any Civil Rights law.

LBJ knew the most virulent racists would never relent, so he went around them and dealt with white lawmakers who needed favors within the system.

When the final vote cleared and the Civil Rights Act became the law of the land, an astonished legion of racists was so angered by the Democratic Party's ode to equal rights they began to make the switch to the Republican Party – which still dominates the South and supports the Sons of the South.

Embrace Technology

One of our most important "crossovers" should be to stop wasting so much of our brainpower and embrace technology – computer science, engineering, math, physics, electronics – as if it were a life preserver thrown to a drowning man.

There were real barriers to technology prior to Civil War III. Our ancestors were barred from pursuing college educations and the few that made it past those barriers were buffeted with resistance. They weren't offered jobs in their fields or they had the fruit of their efforts stolen by white men.

It is only in a society where racism blooms in full can capable people be barred because of their skin color. Hamilton Naki, a South African who grew up during apartheid era, was a laboratory assistant to South African heart surgeon Christiaan Barnard. Despite no formal medical training, much less a college degree, Naki was at the global forefront in organ transplant research.

He is often credited with participating in the world's first human-to-human heart transplant, though that credit was withdrawn by many media outlets.

Whether he was the first to operate on a human heart transplant, or not, it is a fact that his exceptional skills couldn't be denied even by the most blatant of racists. The full flower of black talent hasn't been manifested because, as the Bob Marley song says, they work so hard to 'kill the seed before it grows.'

Our future is in the stars – and that is a literal statement. Technology is now part of human evolution. For the black community to avoid that reality is to choose to walk down an evolutionary dead-end.

Technology will expand our lifetimes, improve our health, sharpen our senses and lead us off this little blue ball that has been all any of us have ever known – but, only if we embrace technology.

"I'm glad I'm black," comedian Richard Pryor joked. "I'd hate to be white because y'all got to go to the moon.

"Ain't no niggers going to the moon, you know that. First of all, there ain't no nigger qualified. Or, so you all tell us."

That is the history of technology up to the second you are reading this. White people decide who will become tech billionaires – surprise! More white people! They decide who to give money to create more technology; they decide who's accepted by "elite" schools to learn technology manipulation and decide on their partners to sell that technology.

The tech industry fought for years to keep its racial composition a secret from the general public. In 2014, we found out why – white and Asian males make up 90 percent of the workforce. Black men and women comprise a miniscule four percent, with virtually no upper management representation.

Black people aren't part of the technology continuum until it comes time to buy the iPhones, Windows 9s and Androids. We have been America's most consistent consumers even as the future races away from us.

Pryor, again:

"They had a movie [about] the future called 'Logan's Run.' ... There ain't no niggers in it. I said, 'Well, white folks ain't planning for us to be here.'"

Recognize PTSD

Modern psychology has become the hand-servant to four masters: the military, politics and advertising. None of the three has any particular affinity for the black community.

The black community has, in the parlance of psychology, some unresolved issues. One major issue is the issue of post-traumatic stress disorder, or PTSD. In a caring society, there would be concern that much of the black community suffers from PTSD and act on efforts to address it.

Consider the countless black men, women and children who have:
- Experienced race-based violence against themselves or others
- Witnessed friends or relatives killed by the police
- Witnessed friends or relatives killed by gang violence
- Tried to find viable work and were turned away
- Experienced homelessness
- Experienced prolonged hunger

Certainly, white people have some of the same experiences, but not even close to the same level as black people. The safety net works very well for white people. Black people have fought Sons of the South dirty tricks since Civil War II. For example, America's biggest societal safety net, Social Security, was set up so as not to include black people.

Right now, there are probably millions of undiagnosed cases of PTSD in the general population of black citizens. To competently diagnose, one has to care. But, there is a singular tough love when it comes to black Americans.

"They can handle it," seems to be the go-to response as the statistics pile on. Early death through heart disease, shrinking middle class, double digit unemployment, growing homeless population, shorter lifespan, police brutality are all minor peccadilloes we must adjust to, say those white people.

Chapter 14
Re-Alpha Black Males

They had me/standing on the front lines/but, now I stand at the back of the line/when it comes to getting ahead -
*— 'Front **Line,**' Stevie Wonder*

Everyone has a breaking point; as does every community. The incidents involving the Freddie Grays, Walter Scotts, Michael Browns, Eric Garners, Tamir Kellys and Trayvon Martins have been piling up for years and only fools would think shooting or killing unarmed young black men with impunity has no psychological effect on the families, friends and community of those young men.

PTSD is just a jumping-off point. There are hundreds of psychological issues which could be studied in specific relation to the black community: colorism, survivor guilt, self-hatred, body image, self-destructive relationships, fear of marriage and countless others.

We require a black psychology, but have been subjected to a young discipline not interested in our stories. Its tools, such as the WAIS or MMPI, have been created with thousands of hours of study of white Americans.

For a scientific discipline, psychology has been embarrassingly incurious about what makes black people tick. Any black man waiting his turn in a barbershop could come up with a dozen avenues of research.

- Why are more black people staying single?
- 'Crabs in a Barrel' – how can we prevent that?
- What effect did passing have on light skinned people?
- What part do the media play in creating anti-black attitudes?
- Why are so many of us so angry with each other?

These are questions most psychologists have no interest in studying because white has been America's default setting. But, when it comes to a purported science of the mind, having white as a default isn't benign, it's criminal behavior because lack of inclusion is the same as a psy-ops attack.

Black psychologists and psychiatrists exist, but they are lone voices in the wilderness. They are not where the money is, so they are on the outskirts of interest.

Dr. Alvin Poussaint remains a strong, steady voice for examining the black psyche, but he suffers the same fate that Sigmund Freud would have suffered if he chose to study black people instead of neurotic Viennese matrons – neglect.

There is always an excuse, in any American social endeavor, when the question of full black participation comes up. In the film industry, if a black feature film is considered for production, the reply is, "Black movies don't sell overseas." In the political realm, before President Obama was elected, pundits were fond of asking black candidates, such as Rev. Jesse Jackson, "What do you want?" As if running for president wasn't answer enough.

Full participation from the black community can only occur when the black community fully participates in its own rebirth.

And, that only comes with a better understanding of the many ways we sabotage our collective efforts – either by being impatient, jealous, afraid of change, too young to know, etc.

Psychology is a young discipline – roughly 125 years old. In just a generation's time, with the help of modern technology and a solid financial investment, the psychological study of black America could be as sturdy and helpful a discipline as the white psychology that exists today.

There is one critical component of any true, effective black psychology, it has to address and help heal centuries of psychological attacks on black males. More directly, its main goal should be to 're-Alpha' black males. If it doesn't address that single issue, it will be a worthless exercise for the black community.

Such a gender-focused strategy may sound chauvinistic, but it is not. It is a pragmatic response to the realities of American society. White males have dominated America since its inception, mostly through means of violently disenfranchising their opponents. American Indians, Asians, Europeans – all males – have been foes in hot wars.

White males never fought wars against white women, they simply excluded them. So, black men are the ultimate opponents for white males.

That 'ultimate opponent' mindset is the source of their fear, a fear that compels white supremacist militias to hide themselves away in the hills and far suburbs and train with guns and bombs, a fear that has white policemen shooting unarmed black men because of phantom threats.

For more than a dozen generations, white males have fought to take away the alpha consciousness, the top dog mentality, of black men.

After enslavement, it was taught by a whip – that demanded we accept its pain – and the sorrowful statement, made after dark while the plantation mistress slept, "There goes master to the slave quarters."

Black alpha males are assertive and aggressive; their instinct is to protect their wives and their families unto death – and millions did die performing that heroic act.

An alpha male, of any color, walks into a new situation and thinks to himself, "I OWN this place." Black men still haven't had that attitude programmed out of their natures, but not for lack of trying on the part of white men.

We are the ultimate opponent for white males because there is an air of mystery about our actions. They wonder, 'Why?'

They question why we haven't them punched them in their noses? Why haven't we burned *white* neighborhoods to the ground?

Time after time, they have provoked us, ala Charles Manson, into starting a race war. They killed our Prince of Retribution, Malcolm X. When that didn't force us into violence, they killed our Prince of Peace, Dr. King.

The only hot war we have waged directly against our oppressors was Civil War I. Our involvement tipped the balance in favor of the North and that angered the Sons of the South. They were defeated by black men they believed they had neutered. Their pride forced them into mental contortions that allowed them to ignore that fact.

"It was a war fought 'on their behalf,' cry the Sons of the South. So, actual war remains on the table in their twisted minds.

Over the course of generations, they and their followers have done all they could to turn black men away from their alpha natures.

What is a black man's nature? To protect his wife and his family; to walk into a situation and think to himself, "I OWN this place."

We need that man. After all, US society has been predicated on protecting the white woman. Who protects the black woman? In films, particularly those made by white people at the height of overt racism, black women were always alone or paired with shiftless husbands. They were sassy maids or child-like servants that no one desired. They had no one who would die for their honor.

Still, despite a trillion dollars worth of brainwashing techniques, black alpha males remain.

There are millions of black men, raised by women, who watch over their families like true alpha males – politely assertive and aggressive when the situation demands.

There are millions who have sublimated their true alpha selves into sports – and not just any sports. The most physical sports of all: football, boxing, basketball, track and field, martial arts.

There are relatively few black men involved in riding, gliding or stick sports. These sublimated alphas crave the full-body experience of showing off their strength, speed, endurance, quickness and toughness. No skates, wheels, rackets, bats or boards for these men. They put their bodies into sweat and blood-soaked competitions against their opponents. It is telling the types of sports most black men populate. They hear the lure of their innate maleness calling.

An honest black psychology would nurture what has been a longtime target for destruction. It would say two things to each successive generation of young black men:

- 'Face your strong black woman. Prove you deserve her.'
- 'Face your white male foe. Defeat him.'

This is a crucial development for the next phase of black society because without it, there will continue to be a devaluation of black life. That translates to continued media frenzies over any missing white girl, while hundreds of little black girls disappear.

Ebola and AIDS vaccines will continue to make their way to white people, while black people die from the diseases.

The media will continue to give voice to those who say unarmed "thugs" like Trayvon Martin, Walter Scott and Eric Garner deserved to die for their respective crimes of buying ice tea and Skittles, running from a police officer and selling single cigarettes without a license.

The science of psychology has done the black community no favors – like most white institutions. But, the harm of its neglect is much more shameful, because it is supposed to be a helping discipline.

Like all systemic racism, the ultimate target is our youth – male and female. They are vulnerable because they are young. They will go through stages of youth that include alternately hating their families, mistrusting advice given in love and seeking their own way.

All of that is relatively benign for white youths because the system offers them a plethora of white-positive images they can attach themselves to as they detach from their families. But, psychologically, our youth are damaged by their natural inclinations.

They are led to believe that white lives are better; that their parents are poor and powerless because of their own weaknesses. And, as we move further away from Civil War II, their young eyes don't see the quotas, roadblocks and other subtle machinations of soft racism that will slowly pull them down until it's too late to resist.

As white Americans start to become a minority demographic, the Great Obama Backlash gathers more steam. What they were once able to accomplish through sheer numbers, they now must achieve through trickery and misdirection.

Some will look to the lessons of apartheid era South Africa to ensure that, even as minorities, their children are uncontested in wielding the nation's power.

It's begun already. Costs for college educations are skyrocketing and states are uninterested in subsidizing their universities. That leaves only the wealthy to attend college – and after the Great Recession, there are far fewer black people in that category. So, education as an equalizer is blocked.

That conservative rush to declare that black and white are at last equal? To scrap anything remotely providing an advantage to black people, such as Affirmative Action, diverse admissions policies? Those behaviors freeze current circumstances, leaving black students and workers at an educational and vocational disadvantage. To maintain a tiered social system, the Sons of the South regularly employ black mouthpieces to supplement white racism.

Some of the Sons' most fervent believers are people such as Ron Christie, a black Republican who bristles at the mention of a "black community."

Christie's words:

"In light of the tragic shooting of Michael Brown [by a white police officer], I've been troubled by the notion that a monolithic entity called 'Black America' or 'the black community' still exists in the 21st century — if it ever existed at all."

He is a black man who is "troubled" by the existence of a black community.

Like white racists who believe only black people are racist, Christie is a Sons of the South-sanctioned black person — similar to Ward Connerly, Clarence Thomas, Michelle Malkin and Jesse Lee Peterson — whose livelihood depends on painting the black community as the aggressors in a centuries-long racial struggle.

Christie took the opportunity created by a white police officer's fatal shooting of an unarmed black teenager to trot out the Sons' party line: the heartfelt desire that the black community never again engage in any collective action for its own betterment.

"The tragedy that took place in Ferguson should have allowed for a meaningful opportunity for everyone in this country to talk about race from an **individual** perspective," Christie wrote in The Daily Beast. "Instead, people who inflame racial tensions to suit their own political ends have helped polarize this nation further, leading to a continued 'us' versus 'them' idea of race that doesn't do justice to our more complicated reality."

In the minds of black people like Christie and Peterson – the latter of whom moaned that white people better wise up or people of color will take over "their" country – organized black people are dangerous. No matter the fact that one of 'them' did kill one of 'us.' Never mind, generally, that white Americans have collectivized for power since the nation was founded, as evidenced by the Continental Congress, labor unions, Masons, the KKK, railroad monopolies, militias, Mothers Against Drunk Driving, the Tea Party and a thousand other collectives up to, and including, the U.S. government.

Apparently, those are the only legitimate communities. If black people have issues, Christie advises, they should do what no other American does – handle it without help.

Christie was particularly incensed in the wake of Brown and Eric Garner (and the 105 black citizens killed by Houston, TX police alone in a five-year period) that the black community decided to take it upon itself to protest.

"… [The] spectacle of Brown's funeral on Monday. The day the young man should have been laid to rest in peace and dignity served as a political pep rally that underscored the false narrative that **something called the black community** is crying out for justice in light of the shooting. NBC News was happy to play into this fantasy in their coverage of Brown's funeral by offering: 'The crowd of 4,500 was brought to its feet by the Rev. Al Sharpton, the activist…who said Brown's killing was a wakeup call for the black community and the entire nation.'"

There are black and white people invested in a Post-Obama Backlash. They are fighting, daily, for continued economic second-class citizenship for black Americans.

Anyone who knows the workplace will understand that 'last hired, first fired' is a generational strategy. Those lucky enough to get high-paying, powerful jobs will try to stay in them for a lifetime and then attempt to pass them along to friends and family.

'You had a black president,' the apologists will say. 'There is no more racism.'

Racism is far from over. It has thrived in the luxury of being overlooked because of young black people's inexperience with it. 'Racism doesn't exist' is the 21st century's most insidious social programming because many of our youths accept it as truth.

They believe it because racism has evolved. Lynch mobs transmogrified into police shootings and 'stand your ground' murders.

They are young, callow and exposed to black people like Christie who deny racism's existence. They spend thousands of hours in a fluffy media cloud of white people who appear friendly and reasonable on their viewing screens. They watch a smattering of non-threatening black actors in tiny, supporting roles telling the white protagonists how much they love them.

So, when parents warn our young boys about very real dangers – dangers that claim thousands upon thousands of young black lives each year – the children see them as out of touch. It's as if they're being told Heinz Doofenshmirtz is going to shank them because of their skin color.

They are the second generation of black people to grow up idolizing a beneficent white man-deity. That first generation was made docile by a billion televised instances of white innocuousness – Howdy Doody, Roy Rogers, Mr. Belvedere, the Fonz, Charles in Charge taught them about white Americans, because most had little firsthand experience with them.

That generation was so pleased to be entertained they forgot the core of their parental duties – to prepare their children for the reality facing them. An entire generation was hoodwinked into thinking neglect was better than hatred.

So, our 21st century youth, insistent that racism is dead, are being taught to covet supporting roles in their own lives; they can drink the Cristal, but not produce it; buy the app, but never write the program; work for the company, but never own it. And, for many, that is perfectly fine.

In the meanwhile, millions of older black men and women see the Devil's Bargain for what it is. With no higher education and no financial legacies passed on, our children will be the high-tech maids and janitors of a new age. They will care for the aging white Baby Boomers until they are gone and then toil for Baby Boomers' babies, slaving away in replaceable industries that evaporate when technology offers up its latest trick. They will struggle in a different way than their elders, but they will still struggle.

Fewer will be murdered by overt racists, but they will be required to know their places. The status quo must hold, cry the Sons of the South.

Do you want to know the level of desperation our young people experience waiting for us to right this ship? Our children are killing themselves, according to recent studies. At every age, black people have traditionally been far less likely to commit suicide than other races. Since 2007 suicides among black children between five and 12 years of age have *tripled*. It is the only age cohort that has a higher suicide rate than its white counterpart.

With a black psychology, we can try and save some of these children, who should be young to know that kind of sorrow a. We can address our shortcomings as a community and identify those black men and women who are mentally predisposed to manifesting self-hatred as hatred of the race.

Most importantly, we can provide a blueprint for our children to be better parents than earlier generations. They will be better able to explain to their children the challenges they will face — without traumatizing them or underestimating their opponents.

That is, after all, part of the job of any real psychology, to help humans deal with their specific problems in adjusting to society. A black psychology will have its work cut out for it.

Chapter 15
Fix the South
You can't run/from Revelations - **'1999,' Prince**

One of the strangest outcomes of Jim Slavery is that its successor racisms are entrenched geographically in the Old South. The sites of some of Civil War III's biggest victories – Brown v. Board, the Selma March, the Montgomery Boycott – are governed at the state level by virtually all-white, Republican politics.

The black Southern electorate is poorer, less educated and unhealthier than its Northern, Eastern and Western counterparts.

There has been greater racial progress in Iowa, with a five percent black population, than in Louisiana with its 40 percent black population. Klansman David Duke ran for office in Louisiana and won a majority of the white male vote. And, there are no repercussions.

This reticence is a problem because the majority of black America lives in the South. Fifty-five percent of Black Americans live in the South, compared to 18 percent in the Midwest, 17 percent in the Northeast and 10 percent in the West.

Florida, Texas and Georgia, combined are home to 10 million black citizens. And, Texas was one of the first states to have its legislators consider seceding from the U.S. after a black man was elected.

What kind of respect is that? What kind of representation is that? America's history was built on the foundation of no taxation without representation. White Southern politicians are not representing black Southern residents.

White Southerners flaunt racial terrorist flags; they try to lie about history by stating the Civil War had nothing to do with slavery; their politicians scheme to deny the vote of black residents; they gerrymander election districts to ensure that black voting power is diluted; in a jailer nation, the South is the biggest jailer and killer of black men, via death penalties.

As a result, the Republican Party, which has been openly combative to the needs of Black Americans (the saying goes, 'Not all Republicans are racist, but all racists are Republican) is solid in the South.

Southern Brothers and Sisters it is imperative that you get your white fellow citizens politically in check. In places like Minnesota, a Muslim black man can be elected to Congress with a majority of white people voting for him against a white candidate. Rep. Keith Ellison has done it.

And, Minnesota is no racial utopia; its black homeownership rates are lower than in Mississippi and its black male incarceration rate is higher. But, politically, anti-black campaigns are non-starters. David Duke need not apply.

Fingers must be pointed, so let's point and be done with it. Southern black people are holding back black ascendance for the 21st century. Until that population copes with its fear of white people/apathy/confusion or whatever keeps it two steps behind in political strategies, our growth will be slowed.

It's not like the remaining 45 percent of black Americans aren't willing to help our Southern brothers and sisters, but fixing the myriad problems starts at home.

There is not enough of a sense of urgency to black politics in the South. Black Southerners' belief that the GOP has won and will always win in the South is a Jim Slavery mentality. It is predicated on a strategy and system to instill hopelessness.

It's related to the hopelessness that Dr. King fought, so it's disappointing that it is still a challenge.

But, the black community doesn't have to win the South overnight. They just have to fight back while others work on an overall strategy. Keep the most virulent racists busy.

More than any other region, the numbers favor the South. There are about 30 million black residents in the region, out of a total Southern population of 115 million. That means about 25 percent of Southerners are black.

One out of four.

That's hardly a minority considering in Civil War III, the Civil Rights Movement, warriors fought and triumphed facing one-against-a-dozen odds.

Dr. King would be licking his chops with those numbers.

And, first things first: politics and judicial appointments are priorities. Black people in the South should be scouted, selected and prepped to do battle in the modern political arena.

If that doesn't happen, Sons of the South will continue to pass 'Stand Your Ground' laws; will continue to pass discriminatory drug sentencing laws; will continue to underfund public schools; will continue to aid anyone seeking to profit off the backs of black Southerners.

Politics is a blood sport, but in the South it is our Thunderdome. Not believing that fact may be reassuring, but it's about as effective as not believing in hypertension. Believe in it or not, it's still going to kill you.

If our Southern brothers and sisters can throw a monkey wrench into the gears of Southern political machinations – push poll, demonstrate, dilute votes, attack bad candidates – we all have a chance for a faster ascendance.

Get racists chasing the terrorist Confederate flag with continual attacks on its existence (it is NOT a symbol of heritage); move into white neighborhoods; target the most racist candidates and picket them; fight to take Rush Limbaugh, Fox News and other hatemongers off the public airwaves, use The Database to select the objects of your boycotts.

Raise hell. Call out EVERY instance of bad behavior into the court of public opinion. Litigate. Engage your rights to civilly disobey.

Do what they do to us – study their behaviors and hit them where they live.

The reason racism is so pernicious is that it has a safe haven in the South. When 25 percent of the South is black, that is more than shameful, it is alarming.

The anti-black racial attitudes of the 20th century need to be pushed further underground and only those who live in proximity can change that.

This challenge, this chapter wouldn't have been written if there was any doubt about what the Black South can do. Black Southerners live in racial hell, but they are sons and daughters of great warriors and they can change that reality.

They should no longer accept having their best and brightest leave home to make it in America. Oprah Winfrey, for instance, had to leave Mississippi and go to Chicago to make her billions.

You black Southerners have the heart. You have the soul. You will be the reason the ascendance succeeds.

Just act.

Chapter 16
Black Rage

Don't do me/no damn favors/I don't know karate/but, I know ka-razor - **'The Payback,' James Brown**

There is an elephant in the room for any discussion of serious black unity – rage. How can we *not* be angry? That is what the Sons of the South and their followers fear most, the eventual reprisal; the other shoe dropping.

They deeply fear black men. That fear is the reason white police and civilians shoot unarmed black men or attack them in mobs. It is the reason many black men are incarcerated so quickly, why black men wait for jobs that never come. Adding financial power to physical power creates an upper-caste that this nation has been resisting for three centuries.

Black men are big; black men are strong, but our violence is largely self-inflicted. We blithely kill each other with guns we have the privilege of buying from white manufacturers.

Still, even a million gladiator-style deaths aren't enough to assuage the fears of millions of white people.

'If they're doing that to each other,' these trembling legions might reason, 'Think what they'll do to us – if they get wise.'

They fantasize about race wars that they could easily lose. Forty-five million pissed-off black people is a nightmare scenario that makes Iran, Iraq and Syria look like the Falklands.

Their fear is logical. After all, who fears an impotent opponent? Still, we accept the psychic violence of systemic racism and heed the advice of those who suggest we continue to accept it.

Here's a reasonable question: 'What the hell?'

Why are we so forgiving to everyone but ourselves? There are groups out there – militias, Klan, certain police forces, certain businesses – who deserve our wrath.

Except for the New Black Panthers, the Five Percenters, the remnants of Blackstone Rangers and a few other non-non-violence groups, we continue to turn all of our cheeks in supplication. This, in a nation that loves its violence and anti-heroes.

White people may have escaped the brunt of our anger, but that fury remains a beast in our community. Our latent rage needs to be re-channeled into something violent, but only deadly when necessary.

We need a 'Warriors' School' for our young black men and women who seem 'angry for no reason.' Warrior School would address three concerns: a uniform rite of passage; nurturing alpha males and channeling young black rage.

It would offer extreme physical challenges – self-protection, weapons training, strategy, fitness and an arena to practice those skills against other young warriors. The goal would be to let that youthful rage blast and have our young black men survive. The streets are an unforgiving training ground.

What doesn't kill us makes us stronger, so the saying goes, but our current street warriors have only learned lessons of death and individualism. They can't honor the community because the community contains their rivals. They only feel strength when they tear down or kill a member of the black community. Those are the lessons presently being learned. It's hard to build with one hand as the other hand destroys your efforts. Work together. Love your family. Learn every day. Most importantly, laugh. Racists *hate* to see us laugh.

"You know how black humor started? It started on the slave ships.
Cat was rowing and dude says, 'What you laughin' about?'
"He says, 'Yesterday, I was a king.'" – Richard Pryor

www.ingramcontent.com/pod-product-compliance
Lightning Source LLC
Chambersburg PA
CBHW071528040426
42452CB00008B/925